Grace

**OTHER BOOKS
BY
JOHN G. REISINGER**

Abraham's Four Seeds
But I Say Unto You
Christ, Lord and Lawgiver Over the Church
Our Sovereign God
Tablets of Stone
The Sovereignty of God in Prayer
The Sovereignty of God in Providence
What is the Christian Faith?

Grace

John G. Reisinger

NEW COVENANT MEDIA
5317 Wye Creek Drive, Frederick, MD 21703-6938

phone: 301-473-4694   fax: 301-473-5128   email: moseley@x-press.net

In this book, the author has placed certain words from Scriptural quotations in italics or bold print without individually marking each instance with such words as "italics mine." The reader should be aware, however, that these italics and bold print are not found in the original texts but are added by the author for reasons of emphasis and clarity.

Grace

Copyright © 1999 by John G. Reisinger

ISBN: 0-9660845-6-X

Requests for information should be addressed to:

New Covenant Media
5317 Wye Creek Drive
Frederick, MD 21703-6938

Scripture quotations marked (NIV) are taken from the HOLY BIBLE, NEW INTERNATIONAL VERSION® NIV® Copyright © 1973, 1978, 1984 by International Bible Society. Used by permission. All rights reserved.

All rights reserved. No part of this publication may be reproduced, stored in a retrieval system, or transmitted in any form or by any means—electronic, mechanical, photocopy, recording, or any other—except for brief quotations in printed reviews, without the prior permission of the publisher.

This book is dedicated to:

Rosemary,

*a lady,
who,
for over fifty-three years,
has exhibited much
of that which is described in the
title and contents of this book*

Table of Contents

Introduction i
Preface 1
Chapter One 9
   The Definition of Grace
Chapter Two 19
   Grace As An Attitude In God
Chapter Three 27
   Grace As **Power** *From God*
Chapter Four 33
   We Are Under laws, But Not Under **The Law**
Appendix A 45
   The Root and Soil of Holiness
Appendix B 55
   Of the Law and a Christian

Introduction

Most of the material in this book was first published in *Sound of Grace,*[1] a Bible study paper. We have received many requests to put the material into book form. The basic idea expressed in this material came from a message by Pastor James Gables of Birmingham, Alabama. The basic idea of his sermon was that grace has more than one component and can never be fully understood until this is recognized. This in no way implies that Pastor Gables endorses either this book or the material in it.

Appendix A was taken from an excellent book by Horatius Bonar entitled *God's Way of Holiness*. Bonar really gets to the heart of the issue in this article. He insists that holiness can only grow out of an absolute assurance of salvation.

Appendix B is a short article by John Bunyan entitled *Of the Law and the Christian*. This single article did more to teach me the relationship of the Christian to the law than anything that I have ever read. Bunyan shows that the conscience must be set totally free from the law before holy living is possible. I gladly claim Bunyan as my mentor on the subject as law and grace.

Bonar, Bunyan, and Spurgeon were all opponents of both "easy"-believism and "hard"-believism. Just as we dare not preach Christ as anything less than Lord as well as Savior, so we cannot have poor sinners looking inside of themselves to find sufficient fruit to have assurance of justification. Spurgeon referred to the "white devil of antinomianism and the black devil of legalism" as equal enemies of the gospel of grace.

Our prayer is that many of Christ's sheep will have their souls filled with an understanding of sovereign grace. We pray that many will drink long from the deep well of grace that is found in understanding the amazing grace of God in the New Covenant.

John G. Reisinger, Dillsburg, PA., June, 1999.

---

[1] For a free copy, write to Sound of Grace, 5317 Wye Creek Drive, Frederick, MD, 21703-6938.

Preface

Learning begins with clear definitions. Until we can define something clearly, it is doubtful that we really understand what we are talking about. If the people who hear us do not understand and agree with our definitions, they will often hear the exact opposite of what we are actually saying. Some years ago the following dialogue took place between an angry lady and my brother Ernest:

"You don't believe those awful things that your brother John believes do you?"

"What awful things do you mean?"

"That all babies go to hell."

"No, I do not believe that."

"That some people sincerely want to be saved but God will not save them because they are not one of the elect."

"Oh, my no, I do not believe that."

The lady sighed in relief and said, "I am so glad that you do not agree with your brother John." My brother knew that I did not believe one single thing the woman accused me of believing. When he told me about the incident he said, "John, if you would have met the lady you would have known it was a waste of time to try to explain to her how totally wrong her views were of what you believe." To this day that dear lady probably thinks that my brother and I disagree about the doctrine of election.

Definitions are like the foundations of a building. If the foundation is not square and level, then the whole building will be crooked not only at the bottom but also all the way up to the top. The whole scheme of redemption, just like a building, will lean in whatever direction the foundation is laid.

Basic presuppositions are to thinking and teaching what a foundation is to a building. Until we can lay out our basic presuppositions in a definitive form it is impossible to intelligently communicate or discuss things with any person who disagrees with us. Something may be an "irrefutable fact" to you but the same thing may be utter nonsense to me. The evolutionist will give us many "facts" that are clearly "proven" by the theory of evolution. However, the man has first assumed as a basic presupposition beyond dispute that evolution is a fact. His belief in evolution is what established the supposed truth of all of his "facts." The same things are not facts to me simply because I do not believe his basic presupposition of evolution. The only level on which that person and myself can have a meaningful discussion with each other is on the level of presuppositions. We must start with the foundation or definition. Is evolution a fact or is it an unproven article of faith used by those who consciously reject the God of the Bible?

The world's problem is not a lack of faith. It has *too much faith.* Unfortunately, its great faith is in the wrong person. All men are *committed believers* who *live by faith.* Some men believe *lies* and live their whole life based on those lies. They build the house (in which they will live eternally) on the sand of lies and reject the authority of Scripture which is the only solid foundation of truth. Everything depends on the starting point or the foundation. This is exactly what Jesus meant in Matthew 7:24–28. Some people build their home on the lies of sand and other build them on the rock of truth. A Christian lives by faith in the words and authority of Jesus Christ the Lord. The non-Christian lives by faith in himself and his own absolute authority.

My wife used to have a housecoat with twenty-two buttons. One day (before she had her morning coffee) she put button number one into hole number two. Devil that I am, I watched her go all the way from top to bottom. She had one button left and no more holes. How many mistakes did she make? We would be prone to say one, but in reality she made *twenty-one* mistakes. She had to undo each button and start all over.

Life is exactly the same except we don't get to start over. We may sail along with little or no trouble (my wife did with 21 buttons). It all seems to go so smoothly. Everything seems to fit so well. However, when we reach the end and face God, then it will be seen that *everything* we did was out of whack simply because it was all done for the wrong reason and off the wrong foundation. This is what Proverbs 21:4 means: "An high look, and a proud heart, and the *plowing of the wicked,* is sin." Plowing in itself is not a sin, but when an unbeliever plows he is acknowledging God's faithfulness in the seasons while his heart is in deliberate rebellion against that God. His very plowing is an unconscious act of faith in the very God he seeks to deny.

This same principle of starting everything from the right foundation is also true in any theological discussion. A man once handed me a 200-page book on the subject of predestination. The author's first statement was, "Predestination is like this: A train company chooses to send a train from Pittsburgh to Chicago. That train is 'pre-destined' to arrive at Chicago at a given time. The train company will guarantee you that since the train is predestined to arrive at Chicago, you will also be 'predestined,' or guaranteed, to arrive at Chicago if you are but willing to get on the train. God's predestination is the same. If you will only 'accept Christ with your free will' then God will guarantee that you will be secure until the train reaches its predestinated goal. Once you 'get on the train of grace' you are eternally secure and 'predestined to get to heaven."

Preface

I handed the book back to the man and said, "The book is not true. The author is totally wrong." The man exploded and said, "How do you know? You have not even read the book!" I tried to explain that if the author's definition was wrong, then the *whole book was wrong*. The definition was merely a summation of the whole book, and the rest of the book was a futile attempt to prove the definition was correct. You may give me a 10,000-page book that begins by saying, "The Bible is not really the inspired Word of God," and I will assure you, without reading another word, that the book is garbage! All of the "facts" presented are manufactured by false presuppositions. Unfortunately, most people, like the man who gave me the book on predestination, are not presuppositional thinkers.

It is a "clear fact" that you can be saved and then lose your salvation *if* you believe that free will is the moving cause of your conversion. If your free will can get you saved that same free will can get you lost. What free will begins it can also end. Since I believe free grace, not free will, is the cause of salvation then being saved and lost is not a possibility. Sovereign grace will finish what it begins! To discuss being "saved and lost" without first discussing free will is a waste of time.

Most theological arguments, and most other arguments as well, might just as well be conducted with an unknown sign language or a silent debate. People do not listen to what the other person is saying and as a result they talk past each other. The old Greek debating society has a good rule that should be followed today. No one was allowed to offer any criticism of a speaker's position until he was able to state, to the speaker's satisfaction, exactly what the speaker had actually said. If this rule were followed today many books that use only caricature would never be published.

Most political, philosophic, and worse, most theological discussions are a total waste of time. Two people will be using the identical same words but each person means something different than the other person. The truth that "God's people must be *sanctified holy*" means something entirely different to me than it does to a Charismatic.

Let us begin with a basic text on the subject of grace:

> Be not carried about with divers and strange doctrines. For it is a good thing that the heart be established ["strengthened"—NIV] with grace; not with meats, which have not profited them that have been occupied therein. Hebrews 13:9

If we are to be protected from being led astray in our Christian life, we must have our hearts *"established with grace,"* or as the NIV says, *"strengthened by grace."* At a minimum that implies the following:

1. We need a heart that understands and loves the truth of grace.

2. We must be convinced that grace is the only power that can give us spiritual strength. Neither the law nor self-effort can give spiritual power.

3. We must understand the whole theology of grace.

4. We must understand and apply the means and follow the process whereby the heart is established or strengthened in grace. It is just as essential that we learn exactly how a saint *grows in grace* as it is to know how a sinner is *saved by grace.*

One does not have to listen to many sermons or read many books to discover that there are some very divergent views on the subject of how a Christian grows in grace. There are many "Keys," "Secrets," and "experiences" which guarantee victory and holiness. In this book we are only concerned with two specific views. One view would emphasize the law in the conscience as the God-ordained schoolmaster for saints, and the other view would free the conscience from the law through marriage to Christ.

Let me illustrate what I mean. Suppose a newly married man wanted the love between he and his wife to grow and create genuine faithfulness to each other. Each morning before he left for work, he would remind her that it is her duty not to commit adultery. During a given month, they would study each day the various things that lead up to adultery so she could be fortified against this sin. Would such a climate be the best way to promote love and faithfulness? We are all in total agreement that it is the woman's duty to love her husband and not to commit adultery. We all want to help her achieve that goal. The real question is this: what is the best way to help the wife grow in love and faithfulness in her heart and life? Will constantly reminding her of her duty produce sincere love? Is it possible that 30 days of studying the little things that lead up to adultery might actually plant some seeds in her mind that she would have never thought of?

Suppose instead of the "remember your duty" method the husband, before he left for work, would kiss his wife and remind her of how much he loved her. At ten o'clock he phoned her and said, "I was thinking about you. I thank the Lord constantly for all you have brought into my life. How about we go out for supper to that Chinese restaurant you like so much." Would love and faithfulness have a better chance in the second atmosphere than the first?

The purpose of this book is not to question whether the law is "holy, just, and good." The Holy Spirit has already settled that (Romans 7:12). Nor is the question whether both lost men and saved men must be clearly instructed in the objective commandments of our God-ordained duty. Both our Lord and the disciples give us many examples of "this *do*" and "this *do not.*" We believe the Bible spells out clear duties. We also believe that a failure to press those duties on both sinners and saints is failing to "preach the whole counsel of God."

Preface

Anyone who suggests that we in any way deny these two things is either grossly ill informed or deliberately spreading a lie.

What then is our main purpose? It is clearly stated in the text we used. We want Christians to live holy lives and we believe that is only possible as "the heart of the Christian is established in *grace.*" We believe sin is so awful and powerful that it actually uses the law as an ally. It is the "holy, just, and good" law of God that literally gives the sin its strength—"The sting of death is sin, and the *power of sin* is *the law*" (I Corinthians 15:56). "Without the law, sin is dead" (Romans 7:8). It is the law that awakes and gives sin its awesome power. God gave the law this function for the express purpose of convincing men of the awful depravity of their hearts. The Holy Spirit explicitly states this truth very clearly:

> (9) We also know that law is made *not for the righteous* but for lawbreakers and rebels, the ungodly and sinful, the unholy and irreligious; for those who kill their fathers or mothers, for murderers, (10) for adulterers and perverts, for slave traders and liars and perjurers—and for whatever else is contrary to the sound doctrine (11) that conforms to the glorious gospel of the blessed God, which he entrusted to me. 1 Timothy 1:9–11. (NIV)

How anyone can read those verses and say, "The greatest aid in a believer's sanctification is the law" is beyond me. Do preachers really believe their congregation is made up of *lawbreakers and rebels, the ungodly and sinful, the unholy and irreligious; those who kill their fathers or mothers, murderers, adulterers and perverts, slave traders and liars and perjurers?*

If the goal in preaching is to stir up sin and give it strength then preaching the law in such a way that brings the believer's conscience under the law is the surest way to accomplish that goal! However, if the goal in preaching to God's sheep is to give them spiritual power to be holy, then the one thing you *must not do* is press the law on the conscience.[2] This is exactly what Paul is saying in 1 Timothy 1:9–11 and 1 Corinthians 15:56. Look those verses up and read them carefully. It is one thing to use the law for the express purpose of making someone feel the reality of sin, it is quite another to use the law as the previously mentioned husband did in the hopes that it will produce strength against sin. The last two statements set forth not only the two different views of sanctification we are discussing, but also how clearly different the two views are. To seek to instill all of the true moral commandments of Scripture in the Christian's mind as a revelation of His Father's will is a preacher's duty. To try to put the Christian's conscience under the law in the hopes that the fear of condemnation will move him away from sin is utter folly. When the law has revealed and condemned sin it has fulfilled its duty and reached its limitations. It

---

[2] See John Bunyan's great statement on the law and the conscience on page 55.

cannot produce or promote holiness. It is the "glorious gospel" alone that gives strength against sin.

John Owen, in his great sermon on Romans 6:14 states the same principle:

> First, the law giveth no strength against sin unto them that are under it, but grace doth. Sin will neither be cast out nor kept out of its throne, but by a spiritual power and strength in the soul to oppose, conquer, and dethrone it. Where it is not conquered it will reign; and conquered it will not be without a mighty prevailing power: this the law will, cannot give.
>
> ... [The law is taken] for the covenant rule of perfect obedience: "Do this, and live." In this sense men are said to be "under it," in opposition unto being "under grace." They are under its power, rule, conditions, and authority, as a covenant ... In this sense the law was never ordained of God to convey grace or spiritual strength unto the souls of men. ... It is not God's ordinance for the dethroning of sin, nor for the destruction of its dominion. ... There is, therefore, no help to expected against the dominion of sin from the law..." The law is holy ... just ... good" but can do them no good, as unto their deliverance from the power of sin. God hath not appointed it unto that end. Sin will never be dethroned by it; it will not give place unto law, neither in its title nor its power ..."
>
> Secondly, the law gives no liberty of any kind; it gendereth unto bondage, and so cannot free us from any dominion—not of sin, for this must be by liberty. But this we have also by the Gospel. There is a twofold liberty:—1. Of state and condition; 2. Of internal operation; and we have both by the Gospel.
>
> ... the freedom of the mind from the powerful inward chains of sin, with an ability to act all of the powers and faculties of the soul in a gracious manner. Hereby is the power of sin in the soul destroyed. And this also is given us IN THE GOSPEL."
>
> Thirdly, the law doth not supply us with effectual motives and encouragements to endeavor the ruin of the dominion of sin in a way of duty; which must be done, or in the end it will prevail. It works only by fear and dread ... these things weaken, enervate, and discourage, the soul in its conflict against sin ..."
>
> Fourthly, Christ is not in the law; he is not proposed in it, not communicated by it—we are not made partakers of him thereby. This is the work of grace, of the gospel. In it is Christ revealed; by it he is proposed and exhibited unto us ... [3]

It is noteworthy that Paul, in 1 Timothy 1:9–11, does not set the law before us as the ultimate standard for sound doctrine, righteousness, or holy living. That which is the ultimate standard for describing a truly righteous life, godly behavior, and correct biblical doctrine is the "glorious gospel of the blessed God." Paul tells Christians to "adorn themselves" with the doctrines of the

---

[3] *Works of John Owen,* Vol. 7, (Carlisle, Banner of Truth)pp 642, 543, 544, 550, 551

Preface

gospel and never sends them back to Moses to be clothed in righteousness in either justification or sanctification.

We know too many preachers, whose sincerity we do not question, who are exactly like the husband mentioned earlier. They hope to produce love and faithfulness by a constant reminder of duty. They send the sheep home every week with the rod of Moses on their back. We must hasten to add that we also know some preachers who think that "preaching Christ" is to never mention either laws or duties. These "position only" men-pleasers send their hearers home with an unshakable confidence in an empty profession. They have a twisted view of the Christian life that almost boasts "we are free to do as we please without fear." This later view is probably more dangerous to men's souls because it is more subtle. It is far easier for a true Christian to fall into a legalist mind set than it is for him to fall into a "let's sin that grace may abound" mind set. Likewise, it is easier for a false convert to fall into an antinomian attitude simply because by nature, or rather by *new* nature, a true Christian will always hate sin and love righteousness. The glory of the New Covenant is that it guarantees that the law will be written in the heart of every true child of God. In both Galatians and Romans Paul warns against both legalism and antinomianism but it is obvious which gets the most attention.

It should also be noted that the more sincere a child of God is in his Christian life, the more he realizes the depth of his depravity and guilt. Unless he really grasps in his conscience the glorious truth of justification by faith on the grounds of the imputed righteousness of Christ, it will be very easy to "try harder to please God" as a means of gaining assurance. Such tender sheep are an easy prey for law preachers who use guilt to manipulate and control. The reverse is also true. The more shallow the knowledge of sin, the more the person will excuse his sin and not be concerned about it. He will never see the need of a remedy that actually deals with the power of sin until he see himself as its impotent victim. Such a person is looking for a ministry that never presses duty nor the necessary evidence of a changed life.

I can honestly say, from personal experience and observation of others, that if the above two choices were the only ones, I would rather be a true believer with a legal mind set and joyless life than I would be a false professor with a happy but groundless assurance. I would rather be a Mr. Fearing than I would a Mr. Talkative. Thank God we do not have to settle for either of these choices. The biblical truth of grace assures us of both victory and joy unspeakable. The blessed Son of God delivers us from the "law of sin and death" and the blessed Holy Spirit leads us to enjoy the fruits of the Spirit as we walk in the promises and precepts of His Word.

Chapter One

The Definition of Grace

"Grace is perhaps the most precious word in the Christian's vocabulary. There is not a more dynamic word in all of the theology of redemption. The believer sings about grace, he hopes in grace, he prays for grace, and it is upon grace that he depends for his entire relationship with God." [4]

"Amazing Grace" is probably the most sung hymn that was ever written. Even the secular world became infatuated with it several years ago and it was Number One on the secular hit parade for over twenty weeks. Paul speaks about the gospel of the grace of God" in Acts 20:24, about "standing in grace" in Romans 5:2, and about "falling from grace" in Galatians 5:4. Peter urges us to "grow in grace," and our text exhorts us to be "established in grace." It is obvious that grace is a very key word in the New Testament Scriptures.

It is safe to say that grace is the foundation and efficient cause of every spiritual blessing and eternal possession that a child of God will ever have. Every knowledgeable believer will gladly say, "I am what I am by the grace of God."

The whole theology of salvation in the New Testament Scriptures is a constant contrast between a religion of works based on obedience to the old legal covenant and the religion of grace based on the new gracious covenant established by Christ. The contrast looks like this:

Old Covenant = Law—Works—Sin—Death

New Covenant = Grace—Faith—Righteousness—Life

There are at least seven things that are essential to a correct understanding of the biblical teaching about grace:

One: A biblical definition of grace that covers all of its major elements and their relationship to each other. This is rarely done by preachers and writers.

Two: A biblical view of the awfulness of sin that forms the necessary background that highlights the true nature and power of grace.

---

[4] As mentioned earlier, I am greatly indebted to Pastor Jim Gables for much of the material in this book. The first chapter is, at points, almost taken right out of a message he gave at Franklin, Tennessee in 1991. This in no way whatever means, or implies, that Pastor Gables agrees with either my additions or application of what he said.

Three: A biblical view of the total antithesis of faith and works in either producing, or in any way maintaining, a sinner's standing or relationship with God.

Four: A biblical view of law that shows how completely antithetical law and grace are in their nature, purpose, and power. Texts like John 1:17, Romans 6:14, and Galatians 4:19–31 must be allowed to mean exactly what they say and not be 'theologized' away. Grace must deliver the believer totally and forever from the condemning power of the law. Until the conscience is set free from the law, we have not grasped the reality of justification by grace through faith.

Five: However, grace to be truly biblical must deliver us from the law in such a way that:
- the law is "magnified and made honorable," and
- grace *is* magnified *even more* by showing that grace *can,* and *really does,* accomplish what the law never could, namely the destruction of sin and bringing sinners into the presence of God without fear.

Six: Grace, to be biblical, must produce a real and lasting change in its objects that demonstrates and proves that a particular person is "not under the law" [because they are not producing the works of the flesh, Galatians 5:18–21], but are under grace [because they are producing the fruit of the Spirit, Galatians 5:22, 23].

- Grace that does not dethrone sin and enthrone righteousness is worthless and is only a cheap imitation.
- Grace that does not dethrone law and enthrone Christ is powerless and a counterfeit.
- Grace that cannot dethrone *both* the reign of law and reign of sin simply cannot be biblical grace.

Seven: Look again at that passage in I Corinthians 15:56. "The sting of death is sin; and the strength of sin is the law." To claim I am "not under the law but under grace" while sin is reigning in my life is to totally deny both the power of grace and the validity of God's "holy, just, and good" law. On the other hand, to claim Christ is my Lord while my life is filled with fear and doubt is to misuse the law and deny grace as well as dishonoring Christ and His all-sufficient work of atonement. To attempt to dethrone sin without putting to silence every claim of the law is to attempt to fight both the Devil and the Holy Spirit *at the same time.*

I would summarize what I am trying to set forth as follows:

Grace, to be biblical grace, must:

The Definition of Grace

1. Conquer the effects and power of sin. Sin must be dethroned as king or grace has no power.
2. Sin cannot be dethroned or conquered until the law is totally satisfied and silenced. The reign of sin and the rule of law go hand in hand.
3. Grace must accomplish this mighty work in such a way that:
    A. The holy law of God is magnified and made honorable; and
    B. Grace is even more magnified by accomplishing what the law was too weak to do.

The following quotation from William Romaine sets forth the central truth concerning grace alone being able to sanctify, or conquer sin in a Christian's life. Italics mine.

> True spiritual mortification does not consist of sin not being in thee, nor upon it being put upon the cross daily, nor yet upon its being kept upon it. There must be something more to establish perfect peace in thy conscience; and that is the testimony of God concerning the body of sin. He hath provided for *thy perfect deliverance* from it in Christ. Everything needful for this purpose was finished by Him upon the cross. He was thy Surety. He suffered for thee. Thy sins were crucified with Him, and nailed to His cross. They were put to death when He died: for He was thy covenant-head, and thou wast legally represented by Him, and art indeed dead to sin by His dying to sin once. *The law has now no more right to condemn thee, a believer, than it has to condemn Him.* Justice is bound to deal with thee, as it has with thy risen and ascended Savior. If thou dost not thus see thy complete mortification in Him, sin will reign in thee. *No sin can be crucified in heart or life, unless it be first pardoned in conscience;* because there will be want of faith to receive the strength of Jesus, by whom alone it can be crucified. If it be not mortified in its *guilt,* it cannot be subdued in its *power.* If the believer does not see his perfect deadness to sin in Jesus, he will open a wide door to unbelief; and if he be not *persuaded of his completeness in Christ,* he gives room for the attacks of self-righteousness and legal tempers. If Christ be not all in all, self must still be looked upon as something great and there will be food left for the pride of self-importance and self-sufficiency; so that he cannot grow into the death of Christ in sensible experience, further than he believes himself to be dead to sin in Christ. The more clearly and steadfastly he believes this, as the Apostle did—*I am crucified with Christ*—in proportion will he cleave to Christ, and receive from Him greater power to crucify sin. This believing view of his absolute mortification in Christ, is the *true gospel method of mortifying sin* in our own persons. Read the sixth of the Romans, and pray for the Spirit of revelation to open it to thee. There thou wilt discover the true way to mortify sin. It is by believing that thou art planted together with Christ in His death; from thence only thy pardon flows, from thence only thy daily victory is received, and from thence thy eternal victory will be perfected. (From: *On the*

Walk of Faith, by William Romaine, quoted by Robert Haldane in his commentary on Romans).[5]

All of the above is but another way of saying, the grace of God that comes in the gospel must totally justify us in our conscience without the works of law, and it must sanctify us in our daily lives without the energy of the flesh. A failure of grace to accomplish either of these two things proves a serious defect in our view of grace.

I think I can say without fear of contradiction that biblical grace will make the sinner perfectly satisfied with the work of Christ *for us* and it will also make Christ satisfied with His work *in* us through the Holy Spirit. We must never forget the stake that our Lord Himself has in both our justification and sanctification. His delivering work of redemption is *from* sin and not *in* sin. Grace that can give us salvation while we still remain in sin does not glorify the saving power of Christ and therefore must be considered counterfeit grace.

Definition of Grace

I want to communicate clearly in this book so I will begin by defining the word *grace*. The English word grace comes from the Greek word *Charis*. It is used over 170 times in its various forms in the New Testament Scriptures. I am sure that many who read this are ready to say, "Grace is one word that I can define. Grace is the *unmerited favor of God to hell-deserving sinners."* This definition correctly includes both a positive and negative aspect. Grace, in this definition, is more than just the unmerited favor of God, it is that favor shown to those who have earned and righteously deserve the exact opposite. This is a good definition of *one* aspect of grace, but it is not even close to being a complete definition of grace. Let me illustrate what I mean. Suppose a boy has been extremely bad in his behavior. His mother informs him that he will get none of his weekly allowance nor will he be allowed to go out of the house to play for a week. On the second day of his confinement the boy begins to bombard his mother with a request for a dollar of his allowance to go buy an ice cream cone. He is reminded that he is not allowed out of the house, and if even he were, he has forfeited his allowance by disobedience. The boy continues to pester his mother and she proceeds to get more aggravated. Like most kids, the boy has learned to strike at the most inconvenient times. On the fourth day, Mother is extremely busy doing some of daddy's books. The boy's constant interruptions, crying, and arguing are so distracting that the mother, in total exasperation, gives him a dollar and says, "Shut up and get out of here." The boy certainly received "unmerited favor when he deserved the exact opposite," but the mother did not show grace. Her action was motivated by anger and

---

[5] Robert Haldane, *Romans, Geneva Series of Commentaries,* (Edinburgh, The Banner of Truth Trust, 1996)pp 253, 254

The Definition of Grace

desperation and, unfortunately, at the expense of righteousness. What she did was *dis*graceful and, in the long run, hurtful to the child.

It is true that one clear definition of biblical grace is the "unmerited favor of God that is given to hell-deserving sinners," but the favor is given out of a pure heart of love and not out of frustration and anger. God's grace is grounded in the total satisfaction of His righteousness, and is not, as in the case of the exasperated mother, given at the expense of both truth and true love.

Having said all of the foregoing, we still have a very defective definition of the word grace. We have clearly given *one definition* of grace but have not come close to a full definition. If we let this narrow definition either be the only meaning of grace or the full meaning of grace, we will muddy up the waters. Unfortunately, that is exactly what has been done.

Grace has more than one shade of meaning. It is impossible to give it a single meaning and then interpret every use of the word grace with that meaning. I need only quote two verses to prove my point:

> And the child [Jesus] grew, and waxed strong in spirit, filled with wisdom: and the grace [unmerited favor] of God was upon him (Luke 2:40).

> And the Word was made flesh, and dwelt among us, (and we beheld his glory, the glory as of the only begotten of the Father,) full of grace [unmerited favor] and truth (John 1:14).

Who will say that the "unmerited favor of God" was given to a "hell-deserving sinner" in these two verses? It is almost blasphemy to even use this as an illustration.

The first thing necessary to learn about the word *charis,* or grace, is that there is nothing at all in the meaning of the word itself to denote whether the favor is earned or not earned. Look at two verses in Luke.

> And the angel said unto her, Fear not, Mary: for thou hast found [unmerited] favor [Charis] with God (Luke 1:30).

> And Jesus increased in wisdom and stature, and in [merited] favor [charis] with God and man (Luke 2:52).

The word *favor* in both of these cases is the word *charis,* or grace, but in one case the grace was not deserved while in the other case it was richly deserved. You can see what will happen to the biblical doctrine of grace if we make every single use of the word fit into one narrow definition.

The best way to show the broad meaning of the word grace is to show its varied usage by both secular and biblical writers. Here is Webster's definition of grace:

> grace—1. Favor, kindness, mercy, etc.; an act or exhibition of such favor, etc.; as, to sue for *grace.* 2. *pl.* state of being favored or in favor; as, to be in one's bad

graces. 3. A short prayer in which a blessing is asked, or thanks rendered, at a meal. 5. Virtue; esp., sense of right; graciousness; as, he had the *grace* to refuse. 6. Title given to a duke, duchess, or archbishop, and formerly to the English sovereign. 7. Temporary exemption, as from a penalty, or relief, as by postponement of a settlement; reprieve, as a day or year of *grace.* 8. Attractiveness; charm; easy, natural elegance or harmony; beauty of line, movement, etc. 9. *Eccl.* a. Divine mercy or forgiveness. b. Divine assistance given man for his regeneration or sanctification. c. In full state of grace. State of being pleasing to God because of responsiveness to grace; also, state of the elect.

Notice the 7th meaning that Webster gave to the word *grace.* Imagine a non-believer coming to an evangelical church for the first time. He is told that God forgives sinners by grace. Last week the man's insurance company sent him a notice saying his policy was overdue and they were giving him a 30-day grace period in which to pay the premium. He could say to himself, "Ah, I see what the preacher is talking about. I wonder how long God's grace period is for me to come with a payment for my sin."

The word grace basically means a pleasant, charming, and becoming appearance which attracts a favorable notice or response. A sermon may be delivered with much *grace.* An ice skater may be truly *graceful.* These few examples, along with Webster's nine different usages of the word, shows that grace has a wide range of meanings. This book will attempt to show and expound the three distinct meanings of grace found in Scripture.

First of all, we will see that grace is *an attitude in the heart of God that shows undeserved favor to hell-deserving sinners.* In this sense, grace is the one and only reason that anyone is ever saved. Grace, in this first sense is almost identical to sovereign election.

Secondly, we will look at grace as *a spiritual power that flows from God into a sinner and effects a genuine change in that sinner.* In this sense, grace is the only source of power for either regeneration or sanctification. In this second sense, grace is almost synonymous with the Holy Spirit.

Thirdly, we will show how grace is also *the response, in terms of gratitude, worship and service, that flows out of those who receive grace.* In this sense, grace demonstrates and proves who really is a child of God or recipient of God's grace. Grace that does not effect true worship and holy living is not biblical grace!

Our understanding of grace then must see it as:
1. an *attitude* in the heart of God,
2. a *power* flowing from the throne of God, and
3. a *result* effected in and through redeemed sinners.

The Definition of Grace

We will develop these three concepts in this book.

Here is a very sketchy list of the different English words used in the King James Bible to translate the Greek word *charis*. The secular Greeks used these different meanings in their writings and the writers of the New Testament Scriptures did the same thing. All of the words in ALL CAPITALS are the Greek word *charis*.

Eph 1:6—"...wherein he has made us ACCEPTED in the beloved." It means God has "graced us" in Christ.

2 Corinthians 1:15—"...that you might have a second BENEFIT." We sometimes jokingly say this is a good verse to teach there is a "second blessing." Paul's coming personally would be double favor or gracing.

1 Timothy 4:14—"Neglect not the GIFT that is in thee." The gifts of the Spirit are the graces of the Spirit. The same idea is in II Tim. 1:6—"...stir up the GIFT of God, which is in thee." You can see how easy we could say, "Stir up the grace of God that is in thee."

Acts 24:27—"Pilate willing to show the Jews a PLEASURE." It means, "Do them a favor" or show them grace. The *charis* that Pilate showed is not the *charis* that God has shown to us poor sinners.

Luke 17:9—"Doth he THANK that servant..." No, because the servant has only done his duty. The servant did not earn favor and the master did not choose to show him any. The master could have chosen to pity the tired man and excuse him from his duties but was not in any way obligated to do so. The moment grace, as it is given to sinners, ceases to be totally optional it ceases to be grace. Grace that can be earned in any sense by a sinner is not grace at all.

Look carefully at the next reference because we are going to come to back to this particular aspect and meaning of grace. Romans 6:17—"But God be THANKED, that you were the servants of sin, but you have obeyed from the heart that form of doctrine to which you have been delivered." We are exhorted to grace or favor God. We grace God when we worship and praise Him. Our worship is the effected response of the power of His grace working in us. Grace literally produces a response of grace in us. We cannot produce this response in the energy of the flesh nor can we suppress it when it is produced by the Spirit.

We have already seen how *charis* is often translated by the word favor. We need not look at any more verses. I think we can easily see that the basic meaning of *charis* is *favor*. If we are talking about a mental attitude, it would be called graciousness. If *charis* is shown toward a person, then it is called favor and the context determines whether the favor was earned or not. If *charis* is the emotional response created in the person receiving the *charis,* then it is translated gratitude or thankfulness as we saw in Romans 6:17.

Although grace has broad and elastic meanings, when the word grace is used to show how a holy God relates Himself to guilty hell-deserving sinners, then the word has a very narrow and rigid meaning. It then truly means unmerited favor and it means that the favor is shown to guilty hell-deserving rebels like us only because of the amazing love of God.

If we view the goodness of God as a generic attitude of heart toward His created order, there are several special varieties of His goodness. *Benevolence* is His good or kind favor terminating upon His created order. The care of God for both men and animals is included. *Love* is His good favor terminating upon rational and personal beings. The sun shines on the just and the unjust. *Mercy* is His good favor terminating upon miserable beings. *Grace* is His favor terminating on sinful rebels. Grace is unique and the highest form of His goodness. It is over and beyond anything imaginable by the human mind.

Rome and the Reformers fought over the true meaning of grace, and unfortunately both narrowed its meaning to an emphasis on only one aspect of grace. Look at a key text:

> And lest I should be exalted above measure through the abundance of the revelations, there was given to me a thorn in the flesh, the messenger of Satan to buffet me, lest I should be exalted above measure. For this thing I besought the Lord thrice, that it might depart from me. And he said unto me, *My grace is sufficient* for thee: for *my strength is made perfect in weakness.* Most gladly therefore will I rather glory in my infirmities, that *the power of Christ* may rest upon me (2 Corinthians 12:7–9).

The words "My *grace,*" "My *strength,*" and "the *power of Christ"* are the same thing. Grace, in this text, is not an attitude in God but is something coming out from God and into Paul. It is the power, or strength of God, given to Paul to enable him to bear his weakness. Grace here is a power from God infused into Paul that moves and strengthens him. We all agree that Paul did not earn or deserve this gift from God. However, that is not the point of the passage.

Rome used this definition of grace for the whole New Testament concept of grace. Salvation by grace then meant that God infuses grace into a sinner and enables him to perform good works. God is then able to justify the sinner on the grounds of his works. Salvation is said to be totally by grace since it was God's grace that gave the sinner the power to do the good works. However, with such a definition, salvation in the end is still salvation by human effort and works. Using this definition as the full and consistent meaning of grace, Rome could make Romans 3:24 teach exactly opposite of what it meant. We need only try

The Definition of Grace

fitting Rome's definition of grace into Romans 4:4, 5 to see it is not a full definition.

> Now when a man works, his wages are not credited to him as a gift, but as an obligation. But to him that worketh not, but believeth on him that justifieth the ungodly, his faith is counted for righteousness (Romans 4:4, 5).

Grace was given to us before we had any good works at all. It was given to us while we were still "ungodly" (Romans 4:4, 5). What we are going to see is that not only does grace have three distinct elements, those three elements must not be confused with each other. Rome was clearly correct in seeing that grace is a spiritual power infused into a man's heart. They were very wrong in confusing that with the doctrine of justification which is based totally on the work of Christ. The Reformers correctly emphasized the truth of justification "apart from any works of the law," but they often failed to teach that sanctification was equally by grace apart from any works of the law. We will come back to this point later. For now, we emphasize again, there are three distinct elements of grace, and it is essential that we not confuse these three elements with each other or get them in the wrong order.

In order to see and understand grace in these three different aspects we must see grace in its distinct relationship with two other things. First of all, *grace must be seen against the background of sin*. It is this stark contrast that makes grace shine with glory. Do you want to know how great is God's grace? Look long and carefully at the depth of the pit of guilt and shame out of which grace lifted us.

Secondly, grace to be biblical grace, must be seen as the *total antithesis of law* (remember what we said about "in such a way as to magnify the law"). We must see that the constant contrast in New Covenant theology, especially Paul, is between the sin/law/works/death motif and righteousness/grace/faith/life motif. It is this strong and absolute antithesis that demonstrates the awesome power of grace. Do you want to see the awesome power of grace? Look at the thickness of the chains of sin and the power of death that held you captive and then you begin to see the power of the grace that delivered you.

Let us begin our understanding of grace by seeing it against the background of sin. Pastor Gables said it well:

> Every book needs a preface to introduce its contents to the reader. Every artist needs a background upon which to accentuate his paintings. Every diamond needs a setting to bring out its beauty and accentuate that beauty. So grace needs its preface, its background, and that is found in the utter sinfulness of mankind. He who is not a sinner is not a proper subject of grace!

Let us examine the awful nature of sin before we try to analyze the amazing jewel of God's grace. Let me again quote Pastor Gables:

When a chemist analyzes water, he discovers two basic elements comprising two parts hydrogen and one part oxygen. When a Bible student analyzes the nature of sin, he discovers two basic elements comprising one part "guilt" and the other part "pollution." Guilt is objective, and pollution is subjective. Guilt affects man's legal status or standing before God, and pollution affects his moral character. Guilt makes him punishable by God and pollution makes him offensive to God. Guilt makes him obnoxious to the justice of God, while pollution makes him obnoxious to the holiness of God. Grace, to be effective, must provide a double remedy to remove both of sin's components. It must remove the guilt of sin and give man a new status before God; and it must cleanse away the stain of sin and give him a new nature. The task of grace is to give the sinner both a new standing and a new heart. You see, I have, as a sinner, a two-fold problem. I have a bad record in heaven, and a bad heart on earth. I need a dual change. But such a double change cannot be accomplished by kindness, or love, or mercy. It can only be done by grace. "Be of sin the double cure, cleanse me from its guilt and power–Save from wrath and make me pure."

That is another way of saying that grace must be able to both justify and sanctify. Grace must deal with the *penalty* of sin, and it must also defeat the *power* of sin.

Most everyone will agree, in theory, with what has just been said. Who will deny that we must be both justified and sanctified? The problem and differences arise when we seek to understand exactly how the Holy Spirit accomplishes these two things. More specifically, the differences are magnified when we look at the exact role that both law and grace play in both justification and sanctification. Our understanding of these things determine both the method and content of our preaching to both sinners and saints. To err in one direction is to become an antinomian, and to err in the other direction is to become a legalist.

We differ greatly from the Arminians in our preaching of justification and we differ just as much from many Reformed people, especially some Reformed Baptists, in our preaching of sanctification. We reject the classical mantra, "The law will bring you to Christ to be justified, and Christ will lead you back to the law to be sanctified." We believe such statements leave Moses as the "big man on campus" in the Christian's life and conscience. We totally agree with John Bunyan that Christ alone must occupy that throne. We reject Rome's idea of "infused grace that enables us to do good works as the ground of justification," and we also reject any notion that a Christian's obedience to the law is the ground of his sanctification.

Chapter Two

Grace As An Attitude In God

Let's begin fleshing out our first definition of grace. *Grace, as an attitude in the heart of God, is His unmerited favor to hell-deserving sinners.* We said this aspect of grace is basically the truth of sovereign election. Although we must insist that grace is a word with broad meanings, when the word is used in connection with how a holy God relates Himself to sinful creatures in salvation the word always has a very narrow meaning. It can only mean that attitude in God's heart which sovereignly purposes to choose and save a multitude of ungodly sinners without any help whatsoever from them. I remind you of what I said previously. This is the aspect of grace that the Reformers saw so clearly and the Roman Catholics missed.

Rome insisted that God's grace was infused into the sinner's heart enabling him to do good works. God rewarded those good works with forgiveness and salvation. Since the grace to perform the good works was *infused by God,* the sinner was therefore saved by grace. The Reformers saw this for exactly what it was—a back door justification by man's works. Neither law nor works furnish any ground for justification. Rome was right in seeing that *one aspect* of grace was God putting spiritual power into our heart. They were very wrong in connecting this in any way with the grounds of justification. Luther used Paul's emphatic statements about the total antithesis between salvation by obeying the law versus salvation by grace to refute Rome. Paul insists that the "law is not of faith" but is the exact opposite. It is impossible to be "under the law," in the sense that Paul is using the word "law," without also being under its curse. Any dealings with the law require a perfect "continuing" to obey all things in the law.

> For as many as are of the *works of the law* are under the curse: for it is written, Cursed is every one that continueth not in all things which are written in the book of the law to do them. But that *no man is justified by the law* in the sight of God, it is evident: for, The just shall live by faith. And *the law is not of faith:* but, The man that doeth them shall live in them (Galatians 3:10–12).

For Paul, there must be a 100% separation of law and grace in justification. It is one or the other but cannot be a mixture of the two in the slightest degree. If works are in any way involved, except as an *essential consequence,* then it is not grace.

> Even so then at this present time also there is a remnant according to the election of grace. And *if by grace, then is it no more of works:* otherwise grace is no more grace. But if it be of works, then is it no more grace: otherwise work is no more work (Romans 11:4–6).

Martin Luther called Romans 4:4, 5 the "death knell to all work mongers" and indeed it is. These words, by themselves, would be the highest form of wicked heresy apart from the cross of Christ. Little wonder that the Jew was scandalized by Paul's doctrine of grace. Imagine declaring that the holy God of Israel received and blessed those who did not work and earn it, and worse, those whom God thus received and blessed were ungodly sinners who deserved to go to hell. And even worse yet, He did it all totally apart from any obedience to the law and in spite of their willful disobedience.

> Now to him that worketh is the reward not reckoned of grace, but of debt. But to *him that worketh not,* but believeth on him that *justifieth the ungodly,* his faith is counted for righteousness (Romans 4:4, 5).

We were justified in God's sight before we had done any good works at all. We were forgiven of every sin without any works of the law. We were accepted by God purely on the grounds of His free gift of grace before we ever performed one single good work. This grace was given to us before we were born and it was given totally apart from any foreknown merit on our part. Grace is here the same as sovereign election.

Who hath saved us, and called us with an holy calling, *not according to our works,* but according to *his own purpose and grace,* which was given us in Christ Jesus *before the world began...*(2 Timothy 1:9).

Martyn Lloyd-Jones suggests that we use Romans 4:4, 5 in witnessing the gospel. We should ask people the following questions.

> The first question is, "How does a person get to heaven and do you think you are going to heaven?" The person will answer in many ways, but in almost every case they will add something like this: "You have to honestly work at becoming a Christian. I admit I am not yet perfect and I still commit some small sins, but I am seriously working at improving. I believe God will accept my sincere efforts." At this point, we tell the person, "I assure you that you *will never make it to heaven.* I can also tell that you do not have the slightest idea about how to become a Christian. The very first mark of a true Christian is *he has quit working and started believing.* He has traded works for faith. The text says, 'To him that *worketh not* but *believeth...'"* This does not mean "to the person who is not concerned at all about obeying God," but "to the person who realizes that he can never earn, by his works, the favor of God."

Paul's whole argument is that you must totally divorce grace from works and debt. And that of course means divorcing it from obedience to law as a means of earning merit with God. If I work and earn something (Romans 4:4), then the individual who "pays me what he owes me" cannot possibly be giving me a gift. If I agree to work for $10.00 an hour, the man for whom I am working *owes* me $400.00 after I have worked forty hours. When he gives me a $400.00 check, he is paying a debt that he owes. His action cannot be called gracious because I earned and deserved the $400.00 which he paid to me. However, if I did no work at all and earned absolutely nothing, the man owes me nothing.

Let's add another ingredient. Suppose I not only did no work, but I deliberately broke the windshield in the man's truck, slashed all of its tires, and poured sand in the gas tank, the man would then owe me punishment. I have not only earned no $400 in wages, but in reality I now deserve to go to jail. If the man in question, under those circumstances, decides to forget about the windshield, gas tank, and tires, and, in spite of the fact I did not work a single hour, still gives me $400.00, that would be most gracious. That would be getting a blessing that I never earned and being spared the punishment which I did earn. Until a sinner sees that he must come to God with nothing in his hands but his own sin and guilt, and totally gives up trying to work his way to heaven, he cannot be saved, by grace or otherwise.

The second question Dr. Lloyd-Jones suggests we ask the person is this: "What kind of people does God accept as His children and do you think that you fit that description?" Again, the person may reply many different ways, but at some point they will usually say something like this: "I am not an angel with wings, but I am basically a good person. I am honest and a good parent. I do not go to church as often as you do, but I do go. I always try to follow the golden rule. I believe God will accept me because I am basically a good person." Again, we must tell them that they will never make it to heaven. Romans 4:5 not only describes the first mark of a Christian as "him that *worketh not,*" but it goes on to say that the second mark is that they "believe in him who justifies *the ungodly.*" God only forgives *ungodly sinners.* He has never yet forgiven one single "good person."

I like to shock people into thinking. When anyone starts talking about being good enough to go to heaven, I will say, "Didn't anyone ever tell you that *good people go to hell and bad people go to heaven?* I know for sure I am going to heaven, and I am going because I am bad and not because I am good." I then explain that I am so bad that I cannot pay my debt to God; I cannot work my way into earning His favor. I am without strength or hope because I am so bad. I must trust solely in the blood and righteousness of Christ. The person may not get converted, but I guarantee he will, at least for one moment, think about why Christ died.

I do not want to be repetitious, but we must see grace as totally antithetical to law and works in the matter of justification. This is the only way to avoid pointing sinners to themselves instead of to a risen Christ. There is no need for any *preparationism* if salvation is 100% by grace. However, the moment we allow works or obedience to the law to get involved in any way in justification then we have opened the door to a works mentality and have denied the grace of

God. We are received and forgiven by God only because of the unmerited favor of God's electing grace. It is 100% by faith as opposed to works, and it is 100% grace as opposed to law. It is either/or (cf. Romans11:4–6). This is the first aspect of grace. Grace, in this first sense, is indeed *an attitude in the heart of God* that shows undeserved favor to hell-deserving sinners. In this sense, grace is the one and only reason that anyone is saved. *Grace, in this first sense is almost identical to sovereign election.*

On the surface there is little disagreement among evangelicals up to this point. No evangelical will say, "You must obey the law to be saved." Likewise, no one denies that sinners must be confronted with both the character of God and the sinner's responsibility to "love God with all his heart." In other words, sinners must be convicted of sin and totally convinced that they are lost and cannot save themselves. However, there is great disagreement concerning the content of the message that we preach to sinners in order to effect the conviction that is essential to true conversion. Should we (1) begin our evangelism to sinners by preaching *only the law and* not even mention the cross until we see "credible evidence" that the person realizes he is a sinner? Or, should we (2) immediately preach Christ and His atonement and say, "Only believe and you will be saved."?

A friend of mine recently took management responsibility for a Rescue Mission. He immediately began to preach sovereign grace. His worst opposition came from some of the most hardened drug addicts. They would say, "You are forgetting that we must do our part in salvation." My friend replied, "If your hope depends on you doing *anything at all* then you do not have a ghost of a chance and *you know it.* You even need God's grace to make you honestly *want to be helped.* If sovereign electing grace is not true, then a three-time loser like you does not have a prayer." The moment that awful truth sank into their hearts, their attitude began to change. The results were amazing.

After about a year, one of the men working for the Mission came to my friend and said, "You and I are far apart in our method of helping these addicts. You are making a terrible mistake in your preaching. You must stand these men under Mt. Sinai until they weep. Then, and not until then, do you give them just a wee bit of the message of grace but not too much. That is dangerous. These people cannot be trusted with pure grace."[6] My friend said, "You are right. You and I are very far apart from each other in what the gospel of grace is all about. I will accept your resignation right now."

The problem that is here highlighted concerns the *power* of the grace of God. The problem arises when we think of grace as nothing more than an

---

[6] See Bonar's excellent response to this objection on page 45.

Grace As An Attitude In God

attitude in the heart of God. When this narrow definition of grace, even though totally correct as *one aspect of grace,* is used as the total meaning of grace, a wrong emphasis on law will always follow. Grace will lose any power, in and of itself, to teach and guide a believer. The power and motivation to produce holiness will be turned over to the law. The bottom line concerns texts like the following:

> For the grace of God that bringeth salvation hath appeared to all men, *teaching us* that, denying ungodliness and worldly lusts, we *should live soberly, righteously, and godly,* in this present world; Looking for that blessed hope, and the glorious appearing of the great God and our Savior Jesus Christ; Who gave himself for us, that he might *redeem us from all iniquity,* and purify unto himself a peculiar people, *zealous of good works* (Titus 2:11–14).

Is there a "teaching power" in grace that is not in the law? Can grace alone accomplish in a believer what the law could never accomplish? Or is there no holiness without the law being the teacher? The answers to questions like these is the real issue involved in understanding the relationship of the law of God to the grace of God. You cannot assign the law a job which it does not have the power to accomplish. Unfortunately, this is exactly what the Puritans often did. In reacting to Rome's misuse of texts like 2 Corinthians 12:9, 10 the Puritans had the tendency to deny that grace alone had the power to sanctify. They relied on the law to produce holy living in the saint. Here is a classic example:

> In a day when antinomianism abounds (the view that the directions of the law of God are no longer needed for Christians to grow in holiness)[7] the Puritans were insistent: 'If Moses goes to the gallows then holiness dies with him.' If the 'grace' we have received does not help us to keep the law, we have not received grace. As the Puritan Samuel Bolton once put it, 'The law sends us to the gospel, that we may be justified, and the gospel sends us to the law again to enquire what is our duty being justified... The Puritans knew that the Bible was the unalterable rule of holiness and would never let themselves, or their hearers, forget it. (From: Banner of Truth Magazine, July, 1993, p.12, 13)

The author of that quotation not only mixed apples and oranges, he threw in some bananas and lemons. Let's look at it sentence by sentence starting at the

---

[7] This is not an accurate definition of antinomianism. An antinomian is against all laws and is a law unto himself. We believe a Christian's life is just as much under the directions of objective laws as the author of the quotation. We merely disagree on where the Christian finds the laws which are his ultimate rule of life. We believe the Sermon on the Mount and New Testament Scriptures gives us a higher standard than Moses ever gave. (See our booklet, "Christ, Lord and Lawgiver Over the Church" available from Sound of Grace, P.O. Box 185, Webster, NY 14580). We affirm as strongly as anyone that the believer needs objective revelation, which includes very clear and specific "dos and don'ts," and he finds more than sufficient of these in the teaching of our Lord Jesus Christ, the new Lawgiver.

end. "The Puritans knew that the Bible was the unalterable rule of holiness and would never let themselves, or their hearers, forget it." I hope I never quit believing, or quit reminding all my hearers, that the "Bible" alone "is the unalterable rule of holiness." But what has that got to do with the gospel sending saints back to Moses to learn about holiness? We wholeheartedly agree that 1 Peter 1:16, quoting Leviticus 11:44, means that just as God commanded the Israelites "to be holy" so He commands believers today "to be holy." However, Peter does not, as Samuel Bolton exhorts, send us back to Moses to learn how to be holy. The rest of Leviticus 11:44 concerns defiling ourselves with unclean food. It is obvious that the "holiness" of an Israelite is not the same as the "holiness" of a sheep of Christ.

A Christian is indeed under the "unalterable rule" of the Word of God as it is understood and interpreted by Christ, the new Lawgiver, and His Holy Spirit inspired Apostles. The unalterable rule of holiness in the Bible and the unalterable rule of holiness in a particular theological system is often quite different. The holiness movements, classical fundamentalism, and the New England Puritan Theocracy are only a few examples.

The true attitude of the Puritans toward the power of the law is seen in the sentence, "If Moses goes to the gallows then holiness goes with him." No Moses, no holiness! Only the law can assure holy living in the life of a Christian. What a horribly inferior view of the power of the grace of God found in the New Testament Scriptures! Has this good brother never read 1 Timothy 1:9–11 and Titus 2:1–15? Or has he found some way to get Moses into the second chapter of Titus? My last comment on this quotation concerns the sentence, "If the 'grace' we have received does not help us to keep the law, we have not received grace." We have been emphasizing the truth that grace always produces fruit, and that fruit is worship and obedience. However, we dare not restrict the help that grace gives to be nothing but "helping us obey the law." This is a "law-centered mentality" that undercuts the true power of grace. Grace enables us to love and serve under the new commandment. Grace also will always produce the fruits of the Spirit "against which there is no law" (cf. Galatians 5:18–23). One writer said we were so afraid of the law that we had "Sinaiphobia." I think the writer of this quotation has "Sinai-itis."

In no sense whatever am I suggesting that the Puritans (or we today) were wrong in preaching the commandments of God to both sinners and saints. They are part of the "whole counsel of God" which is "profitable for doctrine, instructing in righteousness, etc." However, preaching the commandments of God is not necessarily the same thing as "preaching the law." When Paul asked the Galatians, who were eager to go back under the law, "Tell me, ye that desire to be under the law, do ye not *hear the law*" (Galatians 4:21), he surely did not just mean, "Did not anyone ever tell you that it was a sin to commit adultery?

Did you never hear that the seventh day was the holy Sabbath and God required you to totally abstain from all work?" You can "hear" all ten "words of the covenant" written on the tables of stone (Exodus 34:27, 28) without ever "hearing the law" in the sense that Paul is using the word.

"Hearing the law" is hearing it in its covenantal promise of life and threat of death. It is hearing the holy law justly condemn you to hell! You have not heard the law until you hear it saying, "Thou shalt not commit adultery, and the moment you do, *you are a dead man.*" The first part of that last sentence, "Thou shalt not commit adultery," is a clear commandment concerning adultery, and it is just as necessary for us today to teach that commandment as it was when it was written on the tables of the covenant (cf. Deuteronomy. 9:9–11) and given to Israel. The second half of the sentence is the just and certain punishment when that commandment is part of the covenant of law, written on tables of stone (cf. Exodus 34:27-29): under which Israel lived. You have not heard the law until you have heard its just and holy curse against the slightest infraction of that law. A Jew could hear that it was his duty to refrain from all physical work on the seventh day, but he never heard the law until he heard, "Remember the Sabbath to keep it holy, and if you so much as pick up a few sticks then you will *be stoned to death."*

In other words, you can hear all of the Ten Commandments without ever hearing the law, and likewise you can hear the law and, just as with the gospel, really *never hear at all.*

Israel did not hear the law when it was given to them at Sinai or they would have never said, "All that the Lord had said we will do." They would have fallen on their faces and said, "Oh, God, this law is indeed holy, just and good. It is a most righteous and fair covenant that you are making with us today. You have every right to impose it upon us and we have every duty to obey it. We acknowledge all of that. However, You know, and we know, that if this law is to be the terms of the life or death relationship between us, we are all dead before the sun goes down. Is there no other way?"

Likewise, you today have never heard the law until you have heard it in your conscience justly condemning you to hell. That is what Paul wanted the Galatians to realize that it meant to "hear," or to be "under the law." The moment they allowed that knife to touch their skin they were committing themselves to keeping every point of the law and they were also coming under its curse. In that act, they were denying Christ and grace as well as going back under the law and its awful curse. To hear the law is to be forever grateful that we are free from the law because we are under the blood of Christ!

Chapter Three

Grace As Power *From God*

Let us now look at the second aspect of grace and see the foregoing truth set forth. We are not now talking about grace as an *attitude in God's heart* towards a lost man, we are now looking at grace as a *power* that flows out of God into a converted person and empowers that person to live in obedience to God's revealed will. We are moving from justification to sanctification. Let us look at several texts:

> And he said unto me, *My grace is sufficient for* thee: for *my strength is made perfect* in weakness. Most gladly therefore will I rather glory in my infirmities, that *the power of Christ* may rest upon me (2 Corinthians 12:7–9).

Now it is obvious that God's grace in this text is more that an "attitude in God's heart." It is a power that flows out from God and into Paul that enables him to act differently. The phrase, "My grace is sufficient" means exactly the same thing as "My strength is made perfect in weakness," and likewise "my infirmities" are set in distinct contrast to the "power of Christ." Let me repeat our definition of the second aspect of grace:

Grace is also *a spiritual power that flows from God into a sinner* that effects a genuine change in that sinner. In this sense, grace is the only source of power for both regeneration and sanctification. In this second sense, grace is almost synonymous with the Holy Spirit.

Several things are important in that definition. First of all, we insist that grace must produce and maintain a real and lasting change in those who profess to have received it. That is another way of saying that the justification that does not produce an ongoing sanctification is not biblical justification. Salvation by grace cannot be reduced to salvation merely from hell. Biblical grace is salvation from sin that turns us to obedience. The goal of those who, in our minds, misunderstand and misuse the law is identical to our goal. We both want to see holy living among God's people. However, as in the case of evangelism, the content of the message we preach in the hopes of producing that holiness is very different than the message of those who emphasize law. This is evident in the second important statement in our above definition.

We believe that *grace alone* is the only power that can produce holy living. You cannot send people home every week with the threat of the law ringing in their ears and expect them to grow in the knowledge of Jesus Christ and His grace. Remember the illustration of the husband who reminded his wife every day that it was her duty to refrain from adultery.

We agree with Lloyd-Jones in his view of Paul's use of the word law. We also agree with his definition of a legalist. All of the emphasis is mine.

> In winding up his first argument in [Romans] chapter 6 he [Paul] had said, 'For sin shall not have dominion over you', and his reason for saying that is, 'for (because) you are not under the law, but under grace'. He seems to glory in that fact. He seems to be striking another blow at the law. He has already knocked it down, as it were, in chapter 5, verse 20; he is now trampling on it. At once his opponents take up the cudgels and say, 'Surely these are very wrong and very dangerous statements to make; surely if you are going to abrogate the law and do away with it altogether, you are doing away with *every guarantee of righteous and holy conduct and behavior.* Sanctification is impossible without the law. If you treat the law in that way and dismiss it, and rejoice in doing so, are you not encouraging lawlessness, and are you not almost inciting people to live a sinful life?' *Law, they believed, was the great guarantee of holy living and sanctification.* [Log that key statement into your mind!] The Apostle clearly has to safeguard himself, and the truth of the gospel, against that particular misunderstanding and charge.
>
> But the Apostle has another particular object in view also, namely, to show that *sanctification by the law is as impossible as was justification by the law.* The theme of the first four chapters of the Epistle is that a sinner can never be justified by the law. He had already summed that up in a great statement in chapter 3, verse 20: 'Therefore by the deeds of the law shall no man be justified in his sight'. There it is stated categorically. Now, here he is saying in effect in chapter 7, 'Therefore by the deeds of the law shall no man be *sanctified in his sight'.* As it is impossible to be justified by the law, it is equally impossible to be sanctified by the law. As we shall see later, he even puts it as strongly as this, that *not only can a man not be sanctified by the law,* but it is actually true to say that *the law is a hindrance to sanctification,* and that it *aggravates the problem of sanctification.* That is the thesis of this 7th chapter; not only can a man not sanctify himself by observance of the law; *the law is even a hindrance and an obstacle to sanctification.* That is his general thesis, the fundamental proposition he sets out to prove; we must keep it very firmly in our minds. (From: *The Law: Its Functions and Limits,* by D. Martyn Lloyd-Jones, Zondervan, pp. 4, 5).

Lloyd-Jones cannot possibly mean that we should never teach people that it is a sin to commit adultery. We surely do not "hinder a man's sanctification" by reminding him that the Word of God commands him to "love God with all his heart." Instructing a Christian in the clear duties that Christ has laid upon him can in no way hurt his Christian life. Such an idea is ridiculous. What then does Lloyd-Jones mean? He means it is futile to lay the law on a saint's conscience in order to make that saint afraid and thus motivate him to be holy. He means it is wrong to preach to God's sheep as if they were hard-hearted sinners instead of tender sheep with a new heart. It is, as Lloyd-Jones says, believing and preaching like a legalist who sincerely believes that only the law can produce holy living. That is to exalt Moses above Christ and trust the law to do what only the power of grace can do. If Lloyd-Jones is right, and I believe he is dead

Grace As Power From God

center, then much Reformed preaching is a great hindrance to the sanctification of many sincere sheep. If the law is indeed a hindrance to sanctification, then to continually lay it on the conscience of the sheep is to help defeat their efforts to be holy.

The third thing of importance in our definition of the second aspect of grace is the statement that "grace, in this second sense, is almost synonymous with the Holy Spirit." Let me demonstrate that from several texts. We have already seen in 2 Corinthians 12:7–9 that *grace* and *power of Christ* mean the same thing. Calvin makes the following comment on this text:

> The term *grace*, here, does not mean here, as it does elsewhere, the favour of God, but by *metonymy*, the aid of the Holy Spirit, which comes to us from the unmerited favour [charis] of God; ...[8]

In other words, grace was a spiritual force in Paul that energized him to act correctly. To say, "Grace enabled me to resist temptation" is the same as saying, "The Holy Spirit enabled me to resist." This strengthening and enabling power of grace is not emphasized sufficiently in modern preaching, especially in Reformed circles. In most Reformed Baptist churches, law alone has the power to teach and give directions. Love and grace are said to be "blind without the law."

Look at several other texts:

> But by the *grace of God I am what I am:* and his grace which was bestowed upon me was not in vain; but I *labored* more abundantly than they all: yet not I, but the *grace of God which was with me* (1 Corinthians 15:10).

It is obvious that you could substitute the words *Holy Spirit* for the word *grace* at the end of the sentence. Grace in the first part of the sentence could possibly mean the love of God in election, but the later part has to do with the powerful effect of that grace in Paul's life. Grace made Paul act in holiness. Charles Hodge says, "The *grace of God,* in this connection, is not the love of God, but the influence of the Holy Spirit..."

We would say, "by God's grace, I was able to forgive him." You are not talking about an attitude in the heart of God, but the power of the Holy Spirit sent from God into your heart. You could just as easily say, "The indwelling Holy Spirit moved me to forgive." This truth, as so much other truth, is spelled out in the confessions of faith but somehow it got lost in preaching and application. As I said earlier, the classic Reformed litany which I heard for many years was, "Moses will drive you to Christ to be justified and Christ will

---

[8] *Commentary on the Epistles of Paul the Apostle to the Corinthians, Vol. II* by John Calvin, *Calvin's Commentaries* Volume XX, translated by John Pringle, (Grand Rapids, Baker Books, 1996)p 377.

lead you back to Moses to be sanctified." I know of no better way to utterly frustrate the working of God's grace, as a power in us, than to follow that unbiblical advice. That is the quickest possible way to get your eyes off Christ and unto your own works. Look at another text:

> For ye know the grace of our Lord Jesus Christ, that, though he was rich, yet for your sakes he became poor, that ye through his poverty might be rich (2 Corinthians 8:9).

In this verse, the word *grace* cannot be talking about an attitude in the heart of God. The text is referring to the manifestation of the *power* of grace. Grace moves and motivates. In the case of Christ, we see the amazing effects of the grace that was in Him. That grace made Him forsake everything and become nothing. The grace that made Him do what He did was more than "unmerited favor to a hell-deserving sinner." As the results of that powerful grace *came to us,* that was indeed unmerited favor to the worst of hell-deserving sinners. However, that grace *in us* in turn *moved us* to holy actions.

It is grace alone that enables sinners to be and do all that God intends. This truth is sadly lost when we define grace as merely an attitude in the heart of God. Grace is God's power in us through the Holy Spirit. We are not only saved by grace, we live and overcome by grace. Too much preaching today gives the lost sinner more grace than it does to the saint. Jerry Bridges is right when he says:

> All true Christians readily agree that justification is by grace through faith in Christ. And if we stop to think about it, we agree that glorification is also solely by God's grace. Jesus purchased for us not only forgiveness of sins (justification) but also eternal life (glorification). But sanctification—the entire Christian experience between justification and glorification—is another story. At best, the Christian life is viewed as a mixture of personal performance and God's grace. It is not that we have consciously sorted it all out in our minds and have concluded that our relationship with God, for example, is based on 50 percent performance and 50 percent grace. Rather it is a subconscious assumption arising from our own innate legalism—reinforced and fueled by the Christian culture we live in.

> Accordingly, our view of the Christian life could be illustrated by the following time line:

Justification	Christian Life	Glorification
Based on Grace	Based on Works	Based on Grace

According to this illustration, our concept of the Christian life is a grace—works—grace sequence. [It is obvious that such a view is really a works view of the Christian life. In reality, in that system, the sinner is given a lot more grace than is the saint.] The principal thesis of this book, however, and the truth I hope to demonstrate is that the illustration should look like this:

Justification	Christian Life	Glorification
Based on Grace	Based on **Grace**	Based on Grace

That is, the entire Christian life from start to completion is lived on the basis of God's grace to us through Christ.[9]

There is no question that Bridges has identified a serious problem in much current preaching and in the lives of many sincere Christians. I believe part of the root cause of the problem involves turning the power to sanctify a Christian over to the law. The empowering work of the Holy Spirit in sanctification has been missing in most Calvinistic circles. Please note what I did, and did not, say. I did *not* say, or in any way imply, that anything less than heartfelt obedience to God is acceptable in biblical sanctification. Nor did I even remotely suggest that we should not earnestly teach saints all of the clear commandments of their heavenly Father. What I said was that just as sinners must be pointed to a risen Savior as their only help and hope of being justified, just so must a saint be directed outside of himself and told to look to that same risen Lord for all of his help and hope of sanctification. I am saying, along with Bridges and Lloyd-Jones, that you cannot be justified by grace and sanctified by the law.

Apart from Antinomians, we all agree about the two-fold nature of saving grace. In our last chapter we emphasized that grace, to be biblical grace, must conquer sin in our life. Pastor Gables said it better than I:

You see, I have, as a sinner, a twofold problem. I have a bad record in heaven, and a bad heart on earth. I need a dual change. But such a double change cannot be accomplished by kindness, or love, or mercy. It can only be done by grace. "Be of sin the double cure, save from wrath and make me pure."

You see then that if we try to press the two components of sin into one, we will inevitably come up with a flawed remedy. If one group of teachers say that all that is needed, is for man's standing to be changed from condemnation to justification, then you end up with a justified man still in love with his polluted character. If another group of teachers say all that is needed, is for man's polluted character to be sanctified into that of holiness, you end up with a man loving righteousness but still condemned for his past debt of sin. In either case you have a warped foundation upon which to build the scheme of redemption. We need a double cure, and that cure is found in the grace of God mediated through Jesus Christ.

Pastor Gables has stated the bottom line. Cut it any way you want to, we must insist that justification and sanctification are *both* essential to biblical salvation. And we must just as strenuously insist that only grace can produce *either* justification or sanctification. I know of many churches filled with the fruits of "easy believism." These people have positive assurance that they are

---

[9] Jerry Bridges, *Transforming Grace*, (Colorado Springs, Navpress, 1991)pp 19, 20

eternally secure regardless of how they live. They fit into Pastor Gable's category of "a [professing] justified man still in love with his polluted character." We believe that such a creature is an impossible hybrid.

Likewise, I know of many churches where sincere people are serious about working on their sanctification. They strive to be holy in God's sight and yet most of them lack any assurance or joy in their life. They fit Pastor Gable's second category. They may not be actually guilty of gross outward wickedness (and therefore be lost), but they constantly feel guilty and have little, if any, assurance of justification. A joyless child of God is also an impossible hybrid.

We must declare that both justification and sanctification are essential to true salvation. However, we dare not hold assurance hostage to good works in any sense. We must never make the fruits of sanctification to be the grounds of finding peace of conscience before God. Our works have no more to do with keeping us saved, or making us more saved, than they helped to save us in the first place. Grace and law must be separated in both cases.

In the next chapter we will see that being "under *laws*" (plural) is not the same as being "under *the law*" (singular). A New Covenant believer is under objective moral commandments just as was Israel. However, he is not under the law in the same sense that Israel was. If these statements confuse you, then you may not have *"heard* the law."

Chapter Four

We Are Under laws, But Not Under The Law

The law of God written on tables of stone at Mount Sinai was neither a suggestion nor good advice. It was absolute law. This is why that law had the clear and sure penalty of death attached to it. I remember hearing preachers, myself included, who insisted that a 65-mile-an-hour speed limit law with no penalties or fines attached to it could not be called "a law." Without a penalty and a police officer to enforce the law by arresting and fining someone driving 75 miles an hour, the sign was merely advice, a request, or a suggestion. It is the penalty aspect that gives any law the true nature of real law. There can be no true law without penalties being attached. I am sure you immediately realize this is the primary reason a child of God can never be under the law or subject to its just penalty aspect.

The terms and penalties of the law given at Sinai were clearly spelled out. The penalty for breaking any of the covenant laws, the Ten Commandments, written on the Tables of Covenant (Deuteronomy 9:9–11) was stoning to death. A whole judicial system was set up to administer strict punishment for not only breaking the terms of the actual covenant, or Ten Commandments (Exodus 34:27, 28), but also for other sins such as putting out a neighbor's eye, etc. (cf. Leviticus 24:17–20). This was strict and righteous law, no mercy or pity was allowed to be shown (cf. Deuteronomy 19:16–21). This was because a breach of the law under Moses was not a crime against society, it was a sin against the covenant God of Israel. It was not merely the law of the land—it was the law of *God*.

There can be no mercy or pity in true law. John Bunyan showed this clearly with his picture of the man with the club (Moses) beating poor Faithful to death. When Faithful pleaded for mercy, Moses replied, "I do not know how to show mercy," and beat him some more. Only the Man with the scars in his hands could make Moses stop the beating.[10] Bunyan was showing that the law, when allowed to reign in the conscience in any covenantal sense, can only condemn anything less than perfection. The purpose of the law as a covenant was not to show man grace but to show him his great *need* of grace. True law cannot show an ounce of grace, it can only bless perfection and curse the slightest infraction. We have often said, "There was not an ounce of grace in the tablets in the Ark

---

[10] I know of some preachers who not only do not help pull Moses off the poor Christian's conscience, but they actually say, "Sic him" and use the full force of the law to beat the poor sheep's conscience to death.

of the Covenant, but it was very gracious of God to give that covenant to Israel to make them see their need of grace." By the way, don't confuse the Ark of the Covenant with the covenant itself. The covenant was the Ten Commandments (cf. Exodus 34:27–29), or Tables of the Covenant (cf. Deuteronomy 9:9–15), and the Ark was the box that housed the tables of the covenant (cf. Hebrews 9:1, 4). The lid of that box was the mercy seat and pictured nothing but pure grace. The blood on that mercy seat hid the sins against the covenant tables in the box. There was no grace in the tablets in the box but there was nothing but grace in the picture of Christ's sacrifice on the lid of the box. Likewise do not confuse the basic covenant document—The Tablets of Stone, Exodus 34:25–27; Deuteronomy 9:9—with the sacrificial system and priesthood that was necessary to administer the covenant (cf. Hebrews 9:1–15).

Everyone must agree that it is impossible to use the word *law* in its legal meaning without having penalties and judges to enforce the penalty. It is also impossible to deny that the nation of Israel was literally put under the law of God at Sinai and was forever thereafter subject to being stoned to death if they deliberately broke any of the covenant laws written on the tables of the covenant. This death penalty was exacted for breaking any of the covenant laws. You could be stoned to death for picking up sticks (cf. Numbers 15:32–36) or lighting a fire (cf. Exodus 35:2, 3) on the Sabbath.

It is the penalty aspect that gives the law the nature and force of law and puts it in a different category than advice or suggestion. Israel, from Exodus Chapter 20 until the coming of Christ, lived with the constant threat of death if they willfully broke the law. They were literally under the law as a covenant of life and death.

A great theological problem arises when we try to understand how a Christian can be under the law of God when, at the same time, he is totally free from any threat of death or condemnation. If we are free from the curse of the law (Galatians 3:13), which means the law cannot touch us in a condemning sense under any circumstance, then how can we be said to be under the law in any sense whatsoever. We know for certain that a true child of God is eternally secure in Christ and can never come into condemnation (Romans 8:1). It is impossible for a Christian, in a judicial sense, to bear the same "under the law" status as the Jew did at Sinai without also being under the same curse and threat of death. In other words, the very thing that gives law the *nature of law*, namely *a just penalty,* is proof positive that a New Covenant believer cannot be under the law in the same sense as Israel was under law.

It would seem, on the surface, logical to assume that since it takes the curse element to give any rule the status of law, and since believers cannot come under a curse, that there can be no such thing as true law (which must include a curse) in a Christian's life. This is absolutely correct if we are talking about true *covenant* law. We must insist, and very strongly, that justification forever frees a believer, in every sense, from ever again being under the law as a covenant of life and death. Justification equals "no condemnation" and "full and unconditional acceptance with God," and such a status demands our total freedom from the law's power to condemn. This is the argument in Romans 6:14, 15.

However, we must be very careful not to go in the opposite direction. This very reasoning led some good men in history to be labeled antinomians by their enemies. It also led them to make some rash and dangerous statements that appeared, on the surface, to justify the criticism against them. Granted, these men were reacting to a totally wrong preaching of the law to the Christian's conscience, but they were nonetheless wrong in making their extreme statements. Some of these men made statements that seemed to imply that they did not believe there were any objective standards, or laws, at all in the Christian's life. They did not actually believe that a Christian is without any objective laws, or standards, under the New Covenant, but they did leave themselves open to that charge by their rash statements. However, their enemies were guilty of deliberately putting the worst possible connotation on the statements. Both these men, and their opponents, kept using the word *law* in two different ways without clarifying their meaning.

Here are some essential facts that must be understood and applied in any discussion on law and grace.

1. Because a believer is not in danger of going to hell if he breaks one of God's commandments (and remember that is exactly what justification teaches), it does not follow:

    A. that grace teaches us that we can sin as much as we like and it does not matter;

    B. nor does it mean that because *the believer personally* does not have to pay the penalty for sins committed today, therefore the penalty somehow is not paid. All of a believer's sin, before and after conversion, must still be borne and paid for by Christ.

2. Because a Christian cannot be punished—by being sentenced to hell—does not mean there are no serious consequences for him when he sins. However, chastisement from the hands of a *loving Father* must never be equated with *judgment from an offended God!*

3. Because the Christian cannot be under the Old Covenant of life and death made with Israel at Sinai does not mean that there are no laws—in the sense of objective standards—in the New Covenant.

The theological problem arises when we enter a discussion about the distinction between "the law" [Ten Commandments or Tables of the Covenant] and "laws" [specific commandments] in relation to a Christian without first clearly defining the terms and their distinction. Any discussion of the law/grace controversy will always have different sides using the same identical word in many different ways. The word *law* will sometimes mean *covenant*, sometimes *commandment*, and other times *objective revelation*. Some people will even attempt to make *law* mean all three things at the same time.

The title for this chapter is, "A Christian is not under *the law* (singular, meaning "covenant"), but he is under *laws*" (plural, meaning objective commandments). This means a Christian is not under the law, in the sense that Israel was, as a *covenant of life and death*. The Christian is, however, under clear objective commandments that are to guide his daily life and motives. A Christian's life is just as much controlled by objective laws, meaning God-given standards, as was an Israelite's. In no sense do we deny that. However, we insist that the Christian's laws, or standards, are *much higher than those given to Israel*. Grace can, and does, demand far more than the laws given to Moses. Grace is, in every way, higher and better than the law given at Mt. Sinai.

The words *the law* does not mean "the sum total of all laws." The words *the law*, when used in Scripture, usually refer to one of two things: (1) The words refer to the law given on the Tablets of the Covenant to the Nation of Israel. In this covenant sense, Israel is the only nation that was ever under the law. (2) The words refer to either part or all of the Scriptures. It often refers to the first five books of the Bible or the whole Old Testament. In this sense Christians are indeed under the law and morally obligated to keep every true moral commandment in the whole of Scripture.

This is almost the same as the old Puritans saying, "The Christian is not under the law as a covenant of life, but he is under the law as a rule of life." They were close to the truth in that statement, but they could never clearly explain what they actually meant. In one sense they could not explain and work out the implications of their statement because they insisted, most strenuously, that Israel was never under a legal covenant of life and death simply because Sinai could not possibly be a *legal covenant of works,* for there could not be a covenant of works after Genesis 3:15. Their system of theology forced them to contend that the Sinai covenant was the same "gracious covenant" made with Adam after he fell. Sinai must be the same covenant of grace that the church is under. Their statement that the law was, "not a *covenant* of life, but a *rule* of life," was, in a sense, nonsense since they did not really believe the Mosaic law ever was a covenant of works. In reality, no one, except Adam, was ever under a legal covenant of works according to the covenant theology of the Puritans. They insisted on bringing the Ten Commandments over into the New Covenant as a rule of life for Christians. Their primary argument being that those commandments were a rule of life for the *redeemed* people of God, meaning Israel, and you cannot put the redeemed church under a covenant of works. Thus they had a built-in problem. They wanted the law to function in a Christian's conscience as a *rule* of life and not as a *covenant* of life as in the case of Israel. However, at the same time they wanted to deny that the law ever was a legal covenant of life and death. Israel had to be under the same covenant of grace that the believers are under today. Therefore the covenant at Sinai had to be "an administration of the Covenant of Grace". They wanted the same law to function as a covenant and a non-covenant at the same time. They wanted to preach the law to sinners as a threat of death [covenant] as a means of convicting them of their lost condition. However, they wanted to do this while also insisting that the law was never intended by God to function as a *covenant* of life and death.

The Puritans wanted the Decalogue to function both as a covenant of life and death with the power to convict lost sinners to see their need of salvation, and also, at the same time as a rule of life for a believer's sanctification. They further confused the issue by trying to make the law perform *both* of these functions to the *same people* at the same time. Little wonder that these men created confusion in the area of law and grace that neither they, nor their heirs, have been able to clarify. We need only read the many meticulous, but still futile, attempts to distinguish between an "evangelical" obedience to the law and a "legal" obedience.

We sincerely believe the Old Covenant (Decalogue) was a legal covenant of life and death. We reject the idea that it was given to a saved people for their sanctification. Israel, for the most part, was a bunch of hard-hearted rebels—not saints. However, we also believe that every one of the laws that formed the terms of that covenant (The Ten Commandments, Exodus 34:27–29) as they are *interpreted and applied in the New Covenant Scriptures by our Lord and His Apostles* are a vital *part* of a Christian's rule of life today. We cannot equate the Ten Commandments as they are *written on the Tablets of the Covenant* with what has been called, without any biblical support, "the unchanging moral law of God." However, the unchanging moral principles *contained* in the Ten Commandments are just as moral and applicable today as they were when God gave them to Moses on the Tablets of Stone at Sinai. We receive those laws, not as they were written at Sinai, but as they are *changed and enlarged* by our Lord and His Apostles in the New Covenant Scriptures.

Justification—The Leading Doctrine

Most people agree that the leading doctrine of the Gospel is the doctrine of justification by faith. Justification is the glorious truth that I am totally free from the just condemnation of the holy law of God. When God declares a believer to be justified, that puts the believer into a positional status that cannot be changed or altered in any way. All the devils in hell and all of the believer's sin cannot change the truth of justification. It is the absolute and unconditional assurance of acceptance with God. Knowing and understanding the truth of justification enables a true child of God to sing the great hymn:

> Free from the law, O happy condition,
> Jesus has died, and there is remission;
> Cursed by the law and bruised by the fall,
> Grace hath redeemed us once and for all.

What are those words teaching? Are they not declaring the wonder of the Gospel of grace? Are we not free from the law's curse because Jesus died and paid our full debt? Do we not have full and free remission of all sin and deliverance from the effects of the fall because Christ has given us a *complete* redemption? Are believers, or are they not, redeemed *once* and *for all?* If those glorious things are true, *and they are,* then why should anyone hesitate to declare them as loudly and clearly as possible? There is not a single word or implication of bad theology in those words. Only a legalist can be afraid of this hymn! Look at the next verse:

> Now we are free—there's no condemnation,
> Jesus provides a perfect salvation;
> "Come unto me," O hear His sweet call,
> Come, and He saves us once for all.

Is being guaranteed there is no condemnation because the atonement has made us totally free from the reach of the law's just and holy demands something to be afraid of? Doesn't Romans 8:1 say the same thing that the hymn is saying? Should we either soft-peddle Romans 8:1 or else hedge it around with a whole bunch of *ifs* and *buts?* Does Christ's work on our behalf provide a *perfect,* meaning total, or complete, salvation that thoroughly satisfies both God's holiness and the believer's conscience? Do not the words of this hymn set forth the blessed gospel of grace that we so deeply love? If these things are true, why should we hesitate to not only love them, but also to broadcast them as loud and far as we can? How could any child of God object to a single word in those two verses of that hymn? Look at the third verse:

> Children of God, O glorious calling,
> Surely His grace will keep us from falling;
> Passing from death to life at His call,
> Blessed salvation once and for all.

Again, these words should make a child of God shout for joy. Are we wrong in believing that grace will finish the job it starts? Should we encourage

God's weak sheep that their ultimate guarantee of not falling away lies totally in their Shepherd's sovereign purpose and power? Or should we, as the older church member in Bonar's article (See page 45), constantly be afraid of joyous assurance? Should we not carefully work out the implications of what it means to actually be a child of God? Or should we do all in our power to make Christians doubt their salvation so they will double their efforts to "keep the law" in the hopes of finding peace of conscience. Lastly, look at the chorus:

> Once for all, O sinner, receive it,
> Once for all, O brother, believe it;
> Cling to the Cross, the burden will fall,
> Christ hath redeemed us once for all.

Would any true lover of God's grace deliberately warn people to reject this as an antinomian hymn and a perversion of the gospel? Would *you* say, "Don't receive this presumptuous nonsense, but keep working as hard as you can and hope that you might finally make it?" Is not the heart of the matter those words about "clinging to the cross"? No one would dare deny that the cross is the *starting point* for the child of God, but do not some preachers lose the cross and exalt Moses in the Christian life? Do not these people appear to be afraid of grace and full assurance? Remember the question is never, "Is it *essential* that a child of God 'work out his salvation' by continuing to persevere in the faith?" The answer to that is always a loud and emphatic "Yes!" The real question is this: "Does the believer work and obey *because of* the assurance of his salvation, or does he work *in order to secure* assurance of salvation?" As Bonar put it, "Which is the *root* and which is the *fruit?*" Grace that does not make us "run in the way of His commandments" is not biblical grace. Likewise, grace that does not fill the believer with the joy of assurance of acceptance with God is not biblical grace. A good root will always produce good fruit. Is law or grace the root that produces holy living in a sheep of Christ?

My friend, the above hymn is pure sovereign grace. It is the gospel that Paul preached. I have heard it mocked and ridiculed by some good men who really do not understand law and grace. Most preachers know, at least intellectually, that the hymn "Free From Law" quoted above is exactly what justification means. However, they get an uneasy feeling when the truth is laid out in such a bold manner (So did some of Paul's hearers—Romans 6:1). The legalist keeps wanting to say "Yes, but," and then qualify, hedge, and guard grace until it is stripped of its power. The hymn, although as biblical as any hymn that was ever written *if it is seen to be talking about the glorious gospel of justification,* nonetheless makes the legalist squirm. Remember what Lloyd-Jones said about the basic foundation of a true legalist's theology—he believes that the *only way* to produce holy living is by planting the law in the Christian's conscience and constantly reminding him of his duty. This will always lead to a believer trying to find assurance of his acceptance with God in the fruits of his sanctification. Such a poor deluded believer will keep looking inside of himself for evidences upon which he can build his assurance instead of looking outside himself to an enthroned Lord for all of his hope. The theology of Paul is to look away from the law and to Christ alone. True holiness grows out of the assurance of acceptance with God, and that acceptance has absolutely nothing to do with either the law or your obedience. It is rooted in the blood and righteousness of Christ alone. The article beginning on page 45, *"The Root and Soil of Holiness,"* by Bonar is really discussing the heart of the law/grace controversy.

A legalist is terrified of a happy believer who consistently exhibits "love, joy, peace" and the other fruits of the Spirit. In the eyes of a legalist such a person is dangerous. The legalist sincerely believes that "really Godly people" are never that overtly happy and joyous. They are seriously working on their sanctification and constantly groaning under their failure to keep the whole law. The occupation of a "serious and growing Christian" is a constant examination of himself with the Ten Commandments to see how well he is progressing in holiness. Since those commandments rightly demand absolute perfection, and the poor soul, despite his sincerity, cannot even come close to sinless perfection, he must therefore always be doubting his salvation. The more sincere he is in his efforts to keep the law, the deeper will be his doubt and despair. He must try harder to obey the commandments in order to prove he is a child of God before his conscience will be quiet. If such a person continues to sit under a ministry that constantly emphasizes nothing but law and duty (please note the word *constantly*), they will be "of all men most miserable."

Spurgeon has given us a description that, sad to say, fits some present day churches. He was preaching on the "Full Assurance of Faith" and answering common objections made by people who feel that full assurance can be dangerous. He sounds like he has just finished arguing with some law-centered elders that I know.

> I have one more class of objectors to answer and I am finished. There is a certain breed of Calvinist, whom I do not envy, who are always jeering and sneering as much as ever they can at the full assurance of faith. I have seen their long faces; I have heard their whining periods, and read their dismal sentences, in which they say something to the effect—"Groan in the Lord always, and again I say, groan! He that mourneth and weepeth, he that doubted and feareth, he that distrusteth and dishonoureth his God, shall be saved." That seems to be the sum and substance of their very ungospel-like gospel. But why is it they do this? I speak now honestly and fearlessly. It is because there is a pride within them—a conceit which is fed on rottenness, and sucks marrow and fatness out of putrid carcasses. And what, say you, is the object of their pride? Why, the pride of being able to boast of a deep experience—the pride of being a blacker, grosser, and more detestable sinner than other people. "Whose glory is in their shame," may well apply to them. A more

dangerous, because a more deceitful, pride than this is not to be found. It has all the elements of self-righteousness in it. (From *"Full Assurance,"* by C. H. Spurgeon, Metropolitan Tabernacle Pulpit, 1861, p. 292).

A true legalist must, because of his own miserable experience, look at the happy believer as a deceived hypocrite.[11] The poor legalist has no assurance and joy despite all his efforts at law keeping, and must, as a result, resent and suspect the happy believer of either hypocrisy or easy-believism. I love Bonar's story about the older church member, who never had experienced real assurance, solemnly warning the new convert. This is the heart of the issue. Must the Christian's conscience be put under the law as a means of securing holy living, or must the conscience be set totally free from the law before there can be true holy living? One of these represent the truth that Paul preached, and the other represents the legalists who opposed him then and now.

It seems to me that the message of the New Covenant is clear on this point. It is the absolute assurance of unconditional acceptance with God on the sole ground of the blood and righteousness of Christ that furnishes the only effective motive for truly holy living. The law is totally ineffective to either produce or sustain a single holy act. We must be totally free from the law before we can sincerely desire to obey the law. We must be forever convinced that the law cannot give us one ounce of strength before we will look to Christ alone for all of our help. All of this is so simple and clear when we let Scripture mean exactly what is says. However, if we really do not believe in the awesome power of grace to accomplish holiness in the believer, then we will say, "Yes, *but* we must still put the Christian's conscience under law." Spoken like a true legalist! Always remember that a legalist has more confidence in law than he does in grace.

What does Romans 6:14 really mean? It means exactly what it says! The Christian is literally *not under the law,* but in contrast, he is *under grace.* The statement is clear if you will just accept it as written. The law, as covenant law, can *neither bless* a child of God *nor can it condemn him.* As Romaine said, "The law has no more right to condemn thee, a believer, than it has to condemn Christ." The law, in no sense whatsoever, can touch the Christian. It has no

---

[11] I trust that no one will get the impression that everyone who differs from us on the law is a legalist. Some of the sweetest and most joyful Christians I know believe the Ten Commandments are the "unchanging moral law of God." These people strive with their whole being to be holy before God. However, they do so because they know God loves them and never in order to get God to love them. It takes far more than theology to make a legalist just as it takes more than theology to make a sweet Christian. There must a vital union with a living Lord. That vital union is not confined to any one theological group.

power to make him holy and it has no power to condemn him. He is free from the law.

Perhaps the best illustration of a Christian's relationship to the law is to compare it to what is known as diplomatic immunity.

When an ambassador from a foreign country, let's say France, comes to the United States, he is totally free from the laws of the USA. It does not matter what he does, he cannot be arrested. If a policeman would stop him for driving 90 miles an hour, all the ambassador need do is show his credentials and the policeman will apologize for stopping him. An ambassador may shoot and kill a person in front of ten witnesses, but he cannot be prosecuted. He literally is not, in any sense whatever, under the law of the USA. The most our government can do is ask the man's country to take him home.

This is also true of the Embassy building. It is not subject to any of the laws of the USA. Even the local fire department cannot enter the building to put out a fire without first getting permission from the ambassador. Diplomatic immunity means the ambassador is *beyond the reach of the laws of the USA*. He is subject only to the laws of his own country. Of course, our ambassadors in other countries also have the same diplomatic immunity.

Some people may say, "Well, if those people can do whatever they want without any fear of punishment, I am sure they must live unruly and riotous lives." Actually, any ambassador worth his salt is always more careful about keeping our laws than many of our own citizens. However, fear of punishment has nothing at all to do with his reason for obeying. Suppose you were riding in a car with an ambassador. You were late for an important meeting and you asked the ambassador to speed it up, and he replied, "I am already going the maximum speed. I do not want to break the law." You would reply, "But you do not have to worry, they cannot give you a ticket because you have diplomatic immunity. You are not subject to our law. What are you afraid of?" If he were a true ambassador he would say, "I am not afraid of anything. However, my job is to represent my government and country in such a way that you, and your fellow citizens, will see what kind of people we are. How I behave has a great effect on your opinion of my country. One of the first things I did when becoming an ambassador to America was to study all your laws so I could consciously obey them in order to impress you with my country's attitude toward you."

That is the exact picture of the Christian. He consciously wants to know God's will so he can obey it. He is not afraid because he knows he is *totally free from the law*; however, the child of God wants his good works to glorify His Father in heaven. The assurance that he is delivered from the law no more makes a Christian ambassador careless about his life than it does a secular ambassador. The only people who have a real problem with this glorious truth are those sincere, but very misguided, people who believe you can produce true holy living by putting the conscience under the law.

The legalist is really not as much concerned with true holy living as he is concerned with seeing the law reigning in its terrible, but just and holy, condemning power. He wants to see people receive the condemnation they rightly deserve. His fear of lawlessness and desire for honoring the law may be correct on the surface, but it often hides an ugly, unhappy, miserable heart. The legalist's answer to antinomianism (anti-law) is a greater emphasis of law. Paul's answer to the same problem, as Bonar shows, is just the opposite. Paul would totally free the believer's conscience from the threat of law and put the conscience under the power of pure grace.

Putting a true ambassador from France under the law of USA would produce less true obedience to our law than diplomatic immunity. A person who would abuse their immunity is not a true ambassador. He is a phony hypocrite and his country would soon disown him. The same thing is true of a person who professes to be a child of God and lives in willful sin. He is as phony as a three-dollar bill. Such a person's problem cannot be solved by applying the law. In actual fact, his problem is not law; his problem is that he was never regenerated and indwelt by the Holy Spirit; his real problem is that he never came under the power of sovereign grace.

A man once said to Spurgeon, "If I believed your doctrine of eternal security, I would live like the Devil." Spurgeon replied, "Of course you would, that's because you are a devil." A true ambassador of France will live like a law-abiding Frenchman because that is what he is and he wants people to know it for his country's sake. An ambassador of Christ will seek with all his strength to live a law-abiding life because he wants his Father in heaven to be glorified. That is what sovereign grace accomplishes in those who truly receive it. Law preaching can never accomplish the same thing in anyone. If your heart does not earnestly want to obey every known duty to God, then your heart is not under grace. If it is, then grace is as much a total failure as is law. Grace makes men and women to be law keepers. Law stimulates sin in a believer (cf. 1 Corinthians 15:56) and actually is used by sin to push him to be a law breaker.

The most joyful and happy people are always the most holy, and likewise, the most holy people are also the most truly contented and happy. This mean that a person professing to love God's grace while living in sin is the worst of liars. Those two things are impossible if grace is "God's power unto *salvation.*" Likewise, it means that a person saying he "loves God's grace" while living in fear, defeat, and morbid doubt, is just as big a liar. Those two things, like the two just mentioned, are impossible unless God's grace is powerless.

Appendix A

The Root and Soil of Holiness
Horatius Bonar[12]

Every plant must have both soil and root. Without both of these there can be no life, no growth, no fruit.

Holiness must have these. The root is 'peace with God'; the soil in which that root strikes itself, and out of which it draws the vital sap, is the free love of God, in Christ Jesus our Lord. 'Rooted in love' is the apostle's description of a holy man. Holiness is not austerity or gloom; these are as alien to it as levity and flippancy. Nor is it the offspring of terror, or suspense, or uncertainty, but peace, conscious peace, and this peace must be rooted in grace, it must be the consequence of our having ascertained, upon sure evidence, the forgiving love of God. He who would lead us into holiness must 'guide our feet into the way of peace' (Luke 1:79). He must show us how we, 'being delivered out of the hand of our enemies,' may serve God without fear, in holiness and righteousness, before Him, all the days of our life' (Luke 1:74,75). He who would do this must also 'give us the knowledge of salvation, by the remission of sins'. He must tell us how, through 'the tender mercy of our God, ... the dayspring from on high hath visited us, to give light to them that sit in darkness and in the shadow of death' (Luke 1:78).

In carrying out the great work of making us holy, God speaks to us, as 'the God of peace' (Rom. 16: 20), 'the very God of peace' (1 Thess. 5:23) and as being Himself 'our peace' (Eph. 2:14). That which we receive from Him, as such, is not merely 'peace with God' (Rom. 5:1), but 'the peace of God' (Phil. 4:7), the thing which the Lord calls 'My peace' (John 14:27), 'My joy' (John 15:11). It is in connection with the exhortation, 'Be perfect,' that the apostle sets down the gracious assurance: 'The God of love and peace shall be with you' (2 Cor. 13:11). 'These things I will that thou affirm constantly,' says the apostle, speaking of 'the grace of God that bringeth salvation', 'the kindness and love of God our Saviour', the 'mercy of God', 'justification by his grace', in order that (such is the force of the Greek) 'they which have believed in God might be careful to maintain good works'. (Titus 3:8).

---

[12] Horatius Bonar, *God's Way of Holiness* (Durham, England, Evangelical Press, 1979) pp 31–45

In this 'peace with God' there is, of course, contained salvation, forgiveness, deliverance from the wrath to come. But these, though precious, are not terminating points; not ends, but beginnings; not the top but the bottom of that ladder which rests its foot upon the new sepulchre wherein never man was laid, and its top against the gate of the holy city. He, therefore, who is contenting himself with these, has not yet learned the true purport of the gospel, nor the end which God, from eternity, had in view when preparing for us such a redemption as that which He has accomplished for the sons of men, through His only begotten Son, 'who gave Himself for us, that He might redeem us from all iniquity'.

Without these, holiness is impossible, so that we may say this at least, that it is through them that holiness is made practicable, for the legal condition of the sinner, as under wrath, stood as a barrier between him and the possibility of holiness. So long as he was under condemnation, the Law prohibited the approach of everything that would make him holy. The Law bars salvation, except on the fulfilment of its claims; so it bars holiness, until the great satisfaction to its claims has been recognized by the individual, that is, until he has believed the divine testimony to the atonement of the cross, and so been personally set free from condemnation. The Law pronounces against the idea of holiness in an unforgiven man. It protests against it as an incongruity and as an injury to righteousness. If, then, a pardoned man's remaining unholy seem strange, much more so a holy man's remaining unpardoned. The sinner's *legal* position must be set to rights before his *moral* position can be touched. Condition is one thing, character is another. The sinner's standing before God, either in favour or disfavour, either under grace or under wrath, must first be dealt with ere his inner renewal can be carried on. The judicial must precede the moral.

Hence it is of pardon that the gospel first speaks to us, for the question of pardon must first be settled before we proceed to others. The adjustment of the relationship between us and God is an indispensable preliminary, both on God's part and on ours. There must be friendship between us, ere He can bestow or we receive His indwelling Spirit; for on the one hand, the Spirit cannot make His dwelling in the unforgiven; and on the other, the unforgiven must be so occupied with the one question of forgiveness, that they are not at leisure to attend to anything till this has been finally settled in their favour. The man who knows that the wrath of God is still upon him, or, which is the same thing practically, is not sure whether it has been turned away or not, is really not in a condition to consider other questions, however important, if he has any true idea of the magnitude and terribleness of the anger of Him who is a consuming fire.

The divine order then is first pardon, then holiness; first peace with God, and then conformity to the image of that God with whom we have been brought

The Root and Soil of Holiness

to be at peace. For as likeness to God is produced by beholding His glory (2 Cor. 3:18), and as we cannot look upon Him till we know that He has ceased to condemn us, and as we cannot trust Him till we know that He is gracious; so we cannot be transformed into His image till we have received pardon at His hands. Reconciliation is indispensable to resemblance; personal friendship must begin a holy life.

If such be the case, pardon cannot come too soon, even were the guilt of an unpardoned state not reason enough for any amount of urgency in obtaining it without delay. Nor can we too strongly insist upon the divine order above referred to: first peace, then holiness—peace as the foundation of holiness, even in the case of the chief of sinners.

Some do not object to a reputable man obtaining immediate peace, but they object to a profligate getting it at once! So it has always been; the old taunt is still on the lip of the modern Pharisee: 'He is gone to be a guest with a man that is a sinner,' and the Simons of our day speak within themselves and say, 'This man, if He were a prophet, would have known who and what manner of woman this is that toucheth Him, for she is a sinner' (Luke 7:39). But what then of Manasseh, and Magdalene, and Saul, and the woman of Sychar, and the jailor, and the men of Jerusalem, whose hands were red with blood? Were they not trusted with a free and immediate peace? Did not the very essence and strength of the gospel's curative and purifying power lie in the freeness, the promptness, the certainty of the peace which it brought to these 'chief of sinners'? 'So you say you have found Christ, and have peace with God?' said one who claimed the name of 'evangelical,' to a poor profligate who, only a few weeks before, had been drawn to the cross. 'I have indeed,' said the poor man. 'I *have* found him, I *have* peace, and I know it.' 'Know it!' said the divine, 'and have *you* the presumption to tell *me* this? I have been a respectable member of a church for thirty years, and have not got peace nor assurance yet, and you, who have been a profligate most of your life, say that you have peace with God!' 'Yes, I have been as bad as a man can well be, but I have believed the gospel, and that gospel is good news for the like of me; and if I have no right to peace, I had better go back to my sins, for if I cannot get peace as I am, I shall never get it at all.' 'It's all a delusion,' said the other. 'Do you think that God would give a sinner like you peace, and not give it to me who have been doing all I can to get it for so many years?' 'You are such a respectable man,' said the other, in unconscious irony, 'that you can get on without peace and pardon, but a wretch like me cannot. If my peace is a delusion, it cannot be a bad one, for it makes me leave off sin, and makes me pray and read my Bible. Since I got it, I have turned over a new leaf.' 'It won't last,' said the other. 'Well, but it is a good thing while it does last, and it is strange to see the like of you trying to take from me the only thing that ever did me good. It looks as if you would be glad to see me going back to my old sins. You never tried to bring me to Christ, and, now when I have come to Him, you are doing all you can to take me away. But I'll stick to Him in spite of you.'

Some speak as if it were imperiling morality to let the sinner obtain immediate peace with God. If the peace be false, morality may be compromised, by men pretending to the possession of a peace which is yet no peace. But, in that case, the evil complained of is the result of the hollowness, not the suddenness, of the peace, and can afford no ground for objecting to speedy peace, unless speedy peace is of necessity false, and unless the mere length of the process is security for the genuineness of the result. The existence of false peace is no argument against the true, and what we affirm is, that true peace can neither be too speedy nor too sure.

Others speak as if no sinner could be trusted with pardon till he has undergone a certain amount of preliminary mental suffering, more or less in duration and in intensity, according to circumstances. It would be dangerous to the interests of morality to let him obtain an immediate pardon and, especially to be sure of it, or to rejoice in it. If the man has been previously moral in life, they would not object to this; but they question the profligate's right to present peace, and protest against the propriety of it on grounds of subtle morality. They argue for delay, to give him time to improve before he ventures to speak of pardon. They insist upon a long season of preparatory conflict, years of sad suspense and uncertainty, in order to qualify the prodigal for his father's embrace, and to prevent the unseemly spectacle of a sinner this week rejoicing in the forgiveness of his sins, who last week was wallowing in the mire. This season of delay, during which they would prohibit the sinner from assuring himself of God's free love, they consider the proper safeguard of a free gospel, and the needful guarantee for the sinner's future humility and holiness.

Is not, then, the position taken up by these men substantially that adopted by the scribes, when they murmured at the Lord's gracious familiarity with the unworthy, saying, 'This man receiveth sinners, and eateth with them.' And is it not in great measure coincident with the opinion of popish divines respecting the danger to morality from the doctrine of immediate justification through simple faith in the justifying work of Christ?[13]

The apostles evidently had great confidence in the gospel. They gave it fair play, and spoke it out in all its absolute freeness, as men who could trust it for

---

[13] When Bishop Gardiner, the popish persecutor, lay dying in 1555, Day, Bishop of Chichester, 'began to comfort him,' says Foxe, 'with words of God's promise, and free justification by the blood of Christ'. 'What,' said the dying Romanist, 'will *you* open that gap?' meaning that inlet of evil. 'To me and others in my case you may speak of it, but open this window to the people, then farewell all good.'

The Root and Soil of Holiness

its moral influence, as well as for its saving power, and who felt that the more speedily and certainly its good news were realized by the sinner, the more would that moral influence come into play. They did not hide it, nor trammel it, nor fence it round with conditions, as if doubtful of the policy of preaching it freely. 'Be it known unto you,' they said, 'men and brethren, that through this Man is preached unto you the forgiveness of sins, and by Him all that believe are justified' (Acts 13:38). They had no misgivings as to its bearings on morality, nor were they afraid of men believing it too soon, or getting too immediate relief from it. The idea does not seem to have entered their mind, that men could betake themselves to Christ too soon, or too confidently, or without sufficient preparation. Their object in preaching it was, not to induce men to commence a course of preparation for receiving Christ, but to receive them at once and on the spot; not to lead them through the long avenue of a gradually amended life to the cross of the Sin-bearer; but to bring them at once into contact with the cross, that so sin in them might be slain, the old man crucified, and a life of true morality begun. As the strongest motive to a holy life, they preached the cross. They knew that,

'The cross once seen is death to every vice'

and in the interests of holiness they stood and pleaded with men to take the proffered peace.

It is no disparagement to morality to say that good works are not the way to Christ. It is no slighting of the sacraments to say that they are not the sinner's resting-place, so neither is it any deprecation of devotion, or repentance, or prayer, to say that they are not qualifying processes which fit the sinner for approaching the Saviour, either as making the sinner more acceptable or Christ more willing to receive. Still less is it derogating from the usefulness or the blessedness of these exercises, in their proper place and office, to say that they are often the refuges of self-righteousness, pretexts which the sinner makes use of to excuse his guilt in not at once taking salvation from the hands of Jesus. We do not undervalue love because we say a man is not justified by love, but by faith. We do not discourage prayer, because we preach that a man is not justified by prayer, but by faith. When we say that believing is not working, but a ceasing from work, we do not mean that the believing man is not to work, but that he is not to work for pardon, but to take it freely, and that he is to believe before he works, for works done before believing are not pleasing to God.

Is it the case that the sinner cannot be trusted with the gospel?

In one sense this is true. He cannot be trusted with anything. He abuses everything. He turns everything to bad account. He makes everything the minister of sin.

But if he cannot be trusted with the gospel, can he be trusted with the Law? If he cannot be trusted with grace, can he be trusted with righteousness? He cannot be trusted with an immediate pardon; can he be trusted with a tardy one? He cannot be trusted with faith; can he be trusted with doubt? He cannot be trusted with peace; can he be trusted with gloom and trouble? He cannot be trusted with assurance; can he be trusted with suspense, and will uncertainty do for him what certainty cannot?

That which he can, after all, best be trusted with is the gospel. He has abused it, he may abuse it, but he is less likely to abuse it than anything else. It appeals to deeper, stronger, and more numerous motives than all other things together.

The teaching of some in the present day seems fitted, that of others intended, to hinder assurance. Assurance, say some, is impossible. Not impossible, say others, but very hard of attainment; not only very hard, but very long of being reached, requiring at least some thirty or forty years of prayer and good works. Very dangerous, say others, introducing presumption, and sure to end in apostasy. I confess I do not see how my being thoroughly persuaded that a holy God loves me with a holy love, and has forgiven me all my sins, has a tendency to evil (even though I may have reached that conclusion quickly). It seems, of all truths, one of the likeliest to make me holy, to kindle love, to stimulate to good works, and to abase all pride; whereas uncertainty in this matter enfeebles me, darkens me, bewilders me, incapacitates me for service or, at the best sets me striving to work my way into the favour of God, under the influence of a subordinate and mercenary class of motives, which can do nothing but keep me dreading and doubting all the days of my life, leaving me, perhaps, at the close, in hopeless darkness.

Hence the apostles trusted the gospel with the sinner, and the sinner with the gospel, so unreservedly, and (as many in our day would say) unguardedly. 'To him that worketh not, but believeth, his faith is counted for righteousness,' was a bold statement. It is that of one who had great confidence in the gospel which he preached, who had no misgivings as to its unholy tendencies, if men would but give it fair play. He himself always preached it as one who believed it to be the power of God unto holiness, no less than unto salvation.

That this is the understanding of the New Testament, the 'mind of the Spirit', requires no proof. Few would in words deny it to be so; only they state the gospel so timorously, so warily, so guardedly, with so many conditions, terms, and reservations, that by the time they have finished their statement, they have left no good news in that which they set out with announcing as 'the gospel of the grace of God'.

The Root and Soil of Holiness

The more fully that the gospel is preached, in the grand old apostolic way, the more likely is it to accomplish the results which it did in the apostolic days.

The gospel is the proclamation of free love; the revelation of the boundless charity of God. Nothing less than this will suit our world; nothing else is so likely to touch the heart, to go down to the lowest depths of depraved humanity, as the assurance that the sinner has been loved—loved by God, loved with a righteous love, loved with a free love that makes no bargain as to merit, or fitness, or goodness. 'Herein is love, not that we loved God, but that He loved us!' As the lord of the vineyard, after sending servant upon servant to the husbandmen in vain, sent at last his 'one son, his well beloved' (Mark 12:6), so, Law having failed, God has dispatched to us the message of His love, as that which is by far the likeliest to secure His ends. With nothing less than this free love will He trust our fallen race. He will not trust them with Law, or judgement, or terror (though these are well in their place), but He will trust them with His love! Not with a stinted or conditional love, with half pardons, or an uncertain salvation, or a tardy peace, or a doubtful invitation, or an all but impracticable amnesty—not with these does He cheat the heavy laden; not with these will He mock the weary sons of men. He wants them to be holy, as well as safe, and He knows that there is nothing in heaven or earth so likely to produce holiness, under the teaching of the Spirit of holiness, as the knowledge of His own free love. It is not law, but 'the love of Christ', that constraineth! 'The strength of sin is the Law' (I Cor. 15:56), so the strength of holiness is deliverance from the law (Rom. 7:6). Yet are we not 'without law' (1 Cor. 9:21), neither yet 'under the law' (Rom. 6:14), but 'under grace', that we should 'serve in newness of Spirit, and not in the oldness of the letter'.[14]

But so many (it is said) of those who were awakened under the preaching of this very free gospel have gone back, that suspicions arise as to whether it may

---

[14] Thus Calvin writes, 'Consciences obey the Law, not constrained by the necessity of Law, but, being made free from the yoke of Law, they voluntarily obey the will of God. They are in perpetual terror as long as they are under the dominion of the Law, and are never disposed to obey God with delighted eagerness unless they have first received this liberty' *(Inst.* III. xix. 4). 'Not to be under the Law', says Luther 'is to do good and abstain from evil, not through the compulsion of law, but by free love and with gladness.' 'If any man ask me,' says Tyndale, 'seeing faith justifies me, why I work, I answer, love compelleth me; for as long as my soul feeleth what love God hath showed me in Christ, I cannot but love God again, and His will and commandments, and of love work them; nor can they seem hard to me' *(Pref. to Exodus).* 'When faith hath bathed a man's heart in the blood of Christ, it is so mollified that it generally dissolves into tears of godly sorrow; so that if Christ but turn and look upon him, oh, then with Peter he goes out and weeps bitterly. And this is true gospel mourning; this is right evangelical repenting' (Fisher's *Marrow of Modern divinity).*

not be the ultra-freeness of the gospel preached that has produced the evil. It is suggested that, had the gospel been better guarded both before and behind, we should have seen fewer falls and less inconsistency. To this our answer is ready. Multitudes 'went back' from our Lord, yet no one could blame His preaching. There were many grievous corruptions in the early church, yet we do not connect these with apostolic doctrine. Our Lord's parable of the sower implies that, however good the seed might be, and careful the sower, there would be stony-ground hearers and thorny-ground hearers, going a certain length and then turning back. So that the backslidings complained of are such as the apostles experienced, such as our Lord led us to anticipate, under the preaching of His own full gospel.

Further than this, however, we add that, while the preaching of a guarded gospel may lead to no backslidings, it will accomplish no awakenings; so that the question will come to be this: is it not better to have some fallings away when many are aroused, than to have no falling away, because none have been shaken? The question as to what kind of teaching results in fewest backslidings is, no doubt, an important one; but still it is subordinate to the main one: what preaching produces, upon the whole, the most conversions, and brings most glory to God? Apostasies will occur in the best of churches, bringing with them scandal to the name of Jesus, and suspicion of the gospel as the cause of all the evil. But is this a new thing in the earth? Is it not one of the things that strikingly identify us with Corinth, and Sardis, and Laodicea? A minister who has never had his heart wounded with apostasy, who knows nothing of the disappointment of cherished hopes, has too good reason to suspect that there is something sadly wrong, and that the reason of there being no backslidings in his flock, is because death is reigning. Where all is silence or sleep, where the preaching does not shake and penetrate, there will be fewer fallings away; but the reason is, that there was nothing to fall away from. 'Where are your converts now?' was the question put to a faithful minister who had had to mourn the fall of some who once 'ran well'. 'Just where they were: the true still holding fast, the untrue showing themselves.' It was meant as a taunt, but it was a taunt which might have been cast at apostles. It was a taunt which carried comfort with it, as reminding the faithful minister of apostolic disappointment, and so bringing him into fellowship with Paul himself, and as recalling the blessed fact that though some had fallen, more were standing.

The whole Galatian church had lapsed into error and sin. How does the apostle cure the evil?, By fencing or paring down the gospel, and making it less free? No, but by reiterating its freeness; nay, stating it more freely than ever. How free does he represent it in the Epistle! Hence Luther chose it for comment, as the one best suiting himself.

The Root and Soil of Holiness

Some ask the question: 'Is it not a suspicious sign of your gospel, that any of the hearers of it should say, "May we continue in sin, that grace may abound?"?' On the contrary, it is a safe sign of it. Had it not been very like Paul's gospel, it would not have led to the same inquiry with which the apostle's preaching was met. The restricted, guarded, conditional gospel, which some give us, as the ultimatum of their good news, would have suggested no such thought as that which the sixth chapter of Romans was written to obviate. The argument of the apostle, in such a case, becomes unmeaning and superfluous, and hence that statement which prompts some caviller to ask the question: 'Shall we sin, because we are not under the Law, but under grace?' (Rom. 6:15) is not at all unlikely to be the authentic Pauline gospel, the genuine doctrine of apostolic antiquity.

Appendix B

Of the Law and a Christian[15]
John Bunyan[16]

The law was given twice upon Mount Sinai, but the appearance of the Lord, when he gave it the second time, was wonderfully different from that of his [appearance] when at first he delivered it to Israel. [Exodus 19:34]

1. When he gave it the first time he caused his terror and severity to appear before Moses to the shaking of his soul and the dismaying of Israel; [Exodus 19:16; Hebrews 12:18–20] but when he gave it the second time, he caused all his goodness to pass before Moses, to the comfort of his conscience and the bowing of his heart. [Exodus 34:8]

2. When he gave it the first time it was with thunderings and lightnings, with blackness and darkness, with flame and smoke, and a tearing sound of the trumpet; [Exodus 19:16–19] but when he gave it the second time, it was with a proclamation of his name to be merciful, gracious, long-suffering, and abundant in goodness and truth, keeping mercy for thousands, forgiving iniquity, transgressions, and sins. [Exodus 34:6, 7]

3. When he gave it the first time, Moses was called to go up to receive it through the fire, which made him exceedingly to fear and quake; [Exodus 19:18; Hebrews 12:21] but when he went to receive it the second time, he was laid in a cleft of the rock. [Exodus 33:22]

4. From all which I gather that though as to the matter of the law, both as to its being given the first time and the second, it binds the unbeliever under the pains of eternal damnation, (if he close not with Christ by faith,) yet as to the manner of its giving at these two times, I think the first doth more principally intend its force as a covenant of works, not at all respecting the Lord Jesus; but this second time not (at least in the manner of its being given) respecting such a covenant, but rather as a rule or directory to those who already are found in the cleft of the rock, Christ; for the saint himself, though he be without law to God, as it is considered the first or old covenant, yet even he is not without law to him as considered under grace, nor without law to God, but under the law to Christ. [1 Corinthians 9:21]

---

[15] John Bunyan, *The Complete Works of John Bunyan* (Philadelphia; Bradley, Garretson & Co., 1873) pp. 923, 924
[16] All emphasis and material in brackets by JGR.

5. Though therefore it be sad with the unbeliever, because he only and wholly standeth under the law as it is given in fire, in smoke, in blackness, and darkness, and thunder, all which threaten him with eternal ruin if he fulfil not the utmost tittle thereof, yet the believer stands to the law under no such consideration, neither is he so at all to hear or regard it, for he is now removed from thence to the blessed mountain of Zion, to grace and forgiveness of sins; he is now, I say, by faith in the Lord Jesus, shrouded under so perfect and blessed a righteousness that this thundering law of Mount Sinai cannot find the least fault or diminution therein, but rather approveth and alloweth thereof either when or wherever it find it. [Hebrews 12] This is called the righteousness of God without the law, and is also said to be witnessed by both the law and the prophets; even the righteousness of God, which is by faith in Jesus Christ unto all and upon all them that believe, for there is no difference. [Romans 3:22]

6. Wherefore, whenever thou who believest in Jesus doth hear the law in its thundering and lightning fits as if it would burn up heaven and earth, then, say thou, I am freed from this law; these thunderings have nothing to do with my soul; nay, even this law, while it thus thunders and roareth, it doth both allow and approve of my righteousness. I know that Hagar would sometimes be domineering and high even in Sarah's house and against her; but this she is not to be suffered to do, nay, though Sarah herself be barren; wherefore serve it also as Sarah serveth her, and expel her out of thy house. **My meaning is, when this law with its thundering threatenings doth attempt to lay hold on thy conscience, shut it out with a promise of grace; cry, The inn is taken up already, the Lord Jesus is here entertained, and here is no room for the law.** Indeed, if it will be content with being my informer, and so lovingly leave off to judge me, I will be content; it shall be in my sight, I will also delight therein; but otherwise, I being now made upright without it, and that too with that righteousness which this law speaks well of and approveth, **I may not, will not, cannot, dare not, make it my saviour and judge, nor suffer it to set up its government in my conscience; for by so doing I fall from grace, and Christ Jesus doth profit me nothing.** [Galatians 5:1–5]

7. **Thus, therefore, the soul that is married to Him that is raised up from the dead both may and ought to deal with this law of God; yea, it doth greatly dishonor its Lord and refuse its Gospel privileges if at any time it otherwise doth whatever it seeth or feels.** The law hath power over the wife so long as her husband liveth, but if her husband be dead she is freed from that law, so that she is not an adulteress though she be married to another man. [Romans 7:1–3] Indeed, so long as thou art alive to sin and to thy righteousness, which is of the law, so long thou hast them for thy husband, and they must reign over thee. But when once they are become dead unto thee, as they then most certainly will when thou closest with the Lord Jesus Christ, then, I say, thy former

Of the Law and a Christian

husbands have no more to meddle with thee, thou art freed from their law. Set the case: A woman be cast into prison for a debt of hundreds of pounds; if after this she marry, yea, though while she is in the jailer's hand, in the same day that she is joined to her husband her debt is all become his; yea, and the law also, that arrested and imprisoned this woman, as freely tells her, Go; she is freed, saith Paul, from that, and so saith the law of this land. The sum, then, of what hath been said is this: The Christian hath now nothing to do with the law as it thundereth and burneth on Sinai, or as it bindeth the conscience to wrath and the displeasure of God for sin; for from its thus appearing it is freed by faith in Christ. Yet it is to have regard thereto and is to count it holy, just, and good, [Romans 7:12] which that it may do it is always, when it seeth or regards it, to remember that He who giveth it to us is merciful, gracious, long-suffering, and abundant in goodness and truth, &c. [Exodus 34:6]

A 21-DAY DEVOTIONAL
cultivating joy as a fruit of the spirit

His Joy

YOUR STRENGTH

MARILYN HICKEY

Marilyn & Sarah

His Joy Your Strength: Cultivating Joy as a Fruit of the Spirit

Copyright © 2024 Marilyn Hickey Ministries

All rights reserved. No part of this book may be reproduced or transmitted in any form or by any means, electronic or mechanical, including photocopying, recording, or by any information storage and retrieval system, without permission in writing from the publisher.

Marilyn & Sarah Ministries
PO Box 6598
Englewood, CO 80155-6598
marilynandsarah.org

ISBN: 978-1-938696-47-3

Unless otherwise indicated, all Scripture quotations are taken from the New King James Version®. Copyright © 1982 by Thomas Nelson. Used by permission. All rights reserved.

Scripture quotations marked NIV are taken from the Holy Bible, New International Version®, NIV®. Copyright © 1973, 1978, 1984, 2011 by Biblica, Inc.™ Used by permission of Zondervan. All rights reserved worldwide. www.zondervan.com The "NIV" and "New International Version" are trademarks registered in the United States Patent and Trademark Office by Biblica, Inc.™

Scripture quotations marked ESV are taken from The ESV® Bible (The Holy Bible, English Standard Version®), © 2001 by Crossway, a publishing ministry of Good News Publishers. Used by permission. All rights reserved.

Assembled and Produced for Marilyn Hickey Ministries by
Breakfast for Seven
breakfastforseven.com

Printed in the United States of America.

*Come, let us sing for joy to the L*ORD*; let us shout aloud to the Rock of our salvation. Let us come before him with thanksgiving and extol him with music and song. For the L*ORD *is the great God, the great King above all gods.*

PSALM 95:1-3 NIV

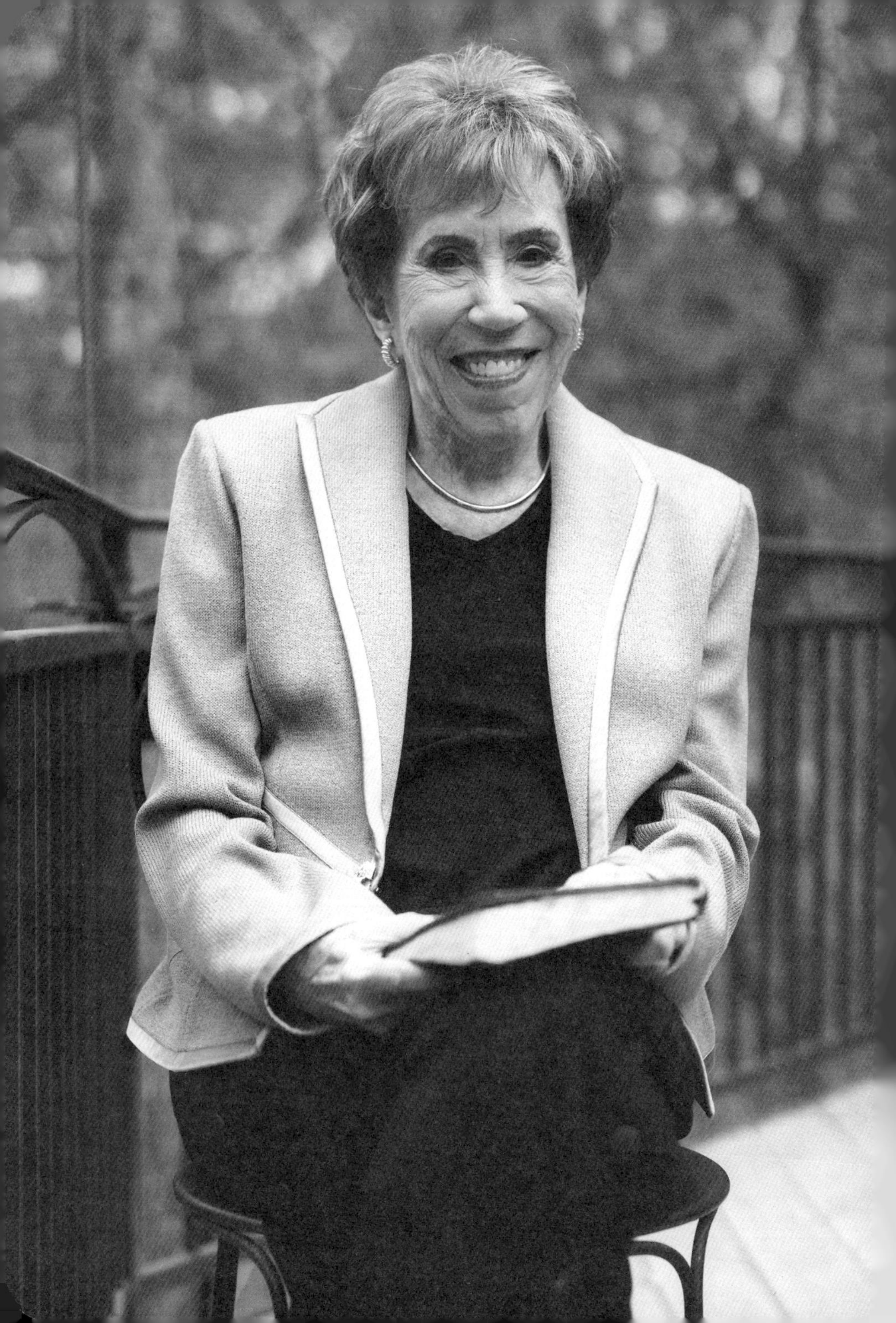

I have fond memories of a song we used to sing to my grandchildren when they were little.

"I've got the joy, joy, joy, joy
down in my heart..."

The next verse...

"I've got the love of Jesus
down in my heart..."

This simple song contains a profound truth of immeasurable value. Joy isn't something that just happens; it comes from Jesus.

To have joy in your heart is rooted in having Jesus as Lord of your heart.

When God's joy is in us, we bear the fruit of love and grace. When we cultivate the joy of the Lord in us, His joy is multiplied to others.

I can't wait to share these next three weeks with you as we discover one of God's greatest gifts, the gift of joy.

From my heart to yours,

Marilyn

Marilyn

But the fruit of the Spirit is love, joy, peace, longsuffering, kindness, goodness, faithfulness, gentleness, self-control. Against such there is no law.

GALATIANS 5:22-23

day one

JOY IS A FRUIT OF THE SPIRIT

Joy is more than happiness. Joy is more than comfort. Joy is more than peace. Joy is so much more than any of these. Joy is a fruit of the Spirit.

The apostle Paul helped form the churches in Galatia and dearly loved the people who were a part of those churches. He believed he had left them in good hands as he extended his mission, but there was corruption taking place, robbing them of their freedom and joy.

Paul wrote a passionate letter to the churches in Galatia. He told them to stick to the gospel as he taught them. He told them not to be in bondage to the former traditions of the Jewish faith, which would serve to rob them of their joy. He told them about the freedom they had in Jesus.

He told them about the "works of the flesh" and the "fruit of the Spirit." The works of the flesh are a burden, while the fruit of the Spirit came with freedom, inspiring those around them.

Joy could never be a burden; it comes from Jesus. Because joy is a fruit of the Spirit, when you have the fullness of the joy of Jesus in you, your joy becomes contagious.

Did you see that? Joy is contagious. When you establish yourself as a person of joy, it affects those around you. When you seek joy for yourself and chase after God with all your heart, circumstances and people around you change.

Choosing JOY

Meditate on Galatians 5:22–23 and ask God to show you the fullness of His joy and how you can bear fruit for your pleasure and His glory.

"These things I have spoken to you, that My joy may remain in you, and that your joy may be full."

―――――
JOHN 15:11

day two

JOY COMES FROM JESUS

Jesus is the source of life, of love, and of joy. It's no surprise that joy is a gift, but it's also a decision. It's not necessarily easy either. But it is so very worth it.

Jesus chose His 12 disciples and spent almost every day and night with them for three years. Yet they struggled to understand Him. Even after seeing Him perform countless miracles and touch thousands of lives, they still tried to fit Him into their own understanding.

Jesus teaches His disciples in the Gospel of John, in the 14th chapter, where He reveals that He is the way, the truth, and the life. He goes on in the 15th chapter to further define what it means to truly abide in Him.

Jesus was always finding new ways to illustrate what it meant to follow Him. In John 15,

He explains that to truly know the Lord is to abide in Him and He to abide in us. It's a relationship so close, Christ defined it with Him as the vine and us as the branches.

When we abide in Jesus, His eternal and unlimited joy is also in us. The Son of God is joy, and therefore, He is the source of our joy. His joy is so abundant, it is sufficient to cover anything this world can try to use to take our joy away.

The secret to having joy in *every* situation is Jesus. When we focus on Him and His strength, His peace, and His provision in us, we will have GREAT joy. We bear fruit when we let His joy overfill us and flow to others.

Choosing JOY

Meditate on John 15:11 and ask God to abide in you, filling you with His joy so strong it remains in you throughout the day.

"For indeed, as soon as the voice of your greeting sounded in my ears, the babe leaped in my womb for joy."

LUKE 1:44

day three

JOY IS THE PRESENCE OF GOD

*E*lizabeth was old and had never been blessed with a child. Her husband, Zacharias, was serving in the temple when an angel visited him with the kind of news that brings joy to one's heart – they were finally going to have a baby. They were to name him "John."

Soon thereafter, Elizabeth became pregnant with a boy.

Mary was young and full of the Spirit of God. An angel visited her and told her she would become pregnant, even though she was a virgin and not yet married. She was to name him "Jesus."

Mary went to visit Elizabeth, who was her cousin, while they were both pregnant. As soon as Elizabeth heard Mary's greeting, her baby, John, leaped in her womb with joy!

Joy is a gift. The very presence of Jesus increases that gift, even if you're just a baby still forming in your mother's womb. How much more can your joy be increased by spending time in the very presence of Jesus?

Joy is a gift, but you receiving that gift is a choice. Choose to spend as much time with Jesus as possible. Your joy will forever increase as you let the presence of Jesus cause your heart to leap with His joy.

Choosing JOY

Meditate on Luke 1:44 and invite God to fully join you, so that your spirit too will leap in His presence.

"I am the true vine, and My Father is the vinedresser. Every branch in Me that does not bear fruit He takes away; and every branch that bears fruit He prunes, that it may bear more fruit."

JOHN 15:1–2

day four

JOY IS ROOTED IN JESUS

In John 15, Jesus teaches His disciples how love and joy are perfected in Him. He begins by explaining that He is the source of all love and joy.

Happiness is something we think we want, but it is usually dependent on external influences. Happiness can come and go. Joy is deeper. Joy is a choice, a deep sense of peace and comfort that transcends what is going on around us, as we rely on Jesus as the source.

Happiness makes us feel good for a moment. Joy, rooted in Jesus, makes us feel loved.

Jesus illustrates that He is the vine, and we are the branches. Through that connection, we prosper and produce fruit. We experience true joy, and our joy is multiplied.

He cultivates us, just like we would plants in our garden. We care and prune and feed them so that they will grow and prosper. Pruning isn't always fun. Sometimes, we look at a plant we just pruned and think, "It looks a little messy." But then the plant begins to grow. And as it grows, it looks better than ever.

Jesus prunes us by taking away anything that separates us from Him. As we are pruned, we are set free from anything that could get in the way of our joy, of His joy in us.

When Jesus abides in our hearts and we abide in Him, we experience the fullness of joy. We grow closer to Jesus, and we are ready for His joy to bloom and prosper. But like any good plant, we can only thrive in connection with our creator and cultivator.

Choosing JOY

Meditate on John 15:1–2 and ask God to show you and take away anything that is in the way of more of His joy.

My brethren, count it all joy when you fall into various trials, knowing that the testing of your faith produces patience. But let patience have its perfect work, that you may be perfect and complete, lacking nothing.

JAMES 1:2-4

day five

JOY IS FOR ALL SEASONS

A few years ago, I fell and broke my hip. I was not happy. It hurt. I spent some time in the hospital, then I had to go to rehab. Rehab hurt too.

We read in the book of James how we are supposed to "count it all joy" when we experience trials in life. So how do we find joy in the struggles, in the pain, in the seasons of hardship?

When I was in the hospital and recovering, I had two options. The first option was to sulk and feel sorry for myself, to let my situation make me unhappy. The second option was to lean into the presence of God and abide in His joy.

The psalmist Asaph tells us in Psalm 77:2, *"In the day of my trouble I sought the Lord."* Do you see that? In a period of testing, he sought the Lord.

I chose option two in my trial. I leaned on Jesus and let Him bring me joy. I was still hurting; I was still uncomfortable, but His presence brought me joy. And His joy brought me peace and a deep comfort in my spirit.

Because I leaned into Jesus, and because He is the source of joy, I was able to experience what Jesus promised in John 16:20, *"Your sorrow will be turned into joy."*

James was right! When you are experiencing the trials in life that are inevitable, Jesus is there to make His joy full in you.

Choosing JOY

Meditate on James 1:2–4 and ask God to fill you so full of joy you can count your trials as blessings.

Restore to me the joy of Your salvation, and uphold me by Your generous Spirit. Then I will teach transgressors Your ways, and sinners shall be converted to You.

PSALM 51:12-13

day six

JOY IN SALVATION

God truly wants each of us to experience the fullness of joy He has for us. We were created to walk in His joy from the beginning. But Adam and Eve chose another path, and it has been a struggle on earth since the fall.

We are born into this separation from God, but we don't have to stay there. Jesus died on the cross to forgive us of our sins, and through Him, our salvation is assured. Think about it — no matter what happens to us in this world, no matter what we do, no matter how much we mess up, we have salvation in Jesus Christ.

This salvation is the ultimate reason to choose joy. When the Lord called me to cover the earth with the Word, He put a very strong burden on my heart. As I stepped into my calling, I felt an unbelievable joy.

It gets better! Not only do I have His joy in my life, but He has been able to produce fruit from my joy. I have gone to countries where women don't even have value, yet I was able to share the love of Jesus. I have also been able to pray for people on airplanes and to receive the joy of Jesus for themselves. I have prayed and shared the joy of salvation with so many people around the world.

Do you see it? The joy of His salvation is for now and for eternity. It takes away the biggest risk in life and gives us the opportunity to rest in His love. It is a joy that multiplies as it is shared with others.

Choosing JOY

Meditate on Psalm 51:12–13 and ask God to restore any joy you are lacking, filling you so full it flows to others.

Looking unto Jesus, the author and finisher of our faith, who for the joy that was set before Him endured the cross, despising the shame, and has sat down at the right hand of the throne of God.

HEBREWS 12:2

day seven

JOY IS MULTIPLIED IN SERVICE

Jesus was fully God, and He was fully man. He knew the power His sacrifice would have on the entirety of the human race, but He did not look forward to the suffering He would endure.

The night before Jesus was crucified, Jesus observed the Passover with His disciples. They broke bread together, they shared wine, and He tried to tell them what was about to happen. They did not understand Him though.

Then, as the hour approached of His arrest, when the gravity of His impending ordeal was almost unbearable, He did something profound. He stripped down, wrapped a towel around His waist, and washed the feet of His disciples.

He served them. He was setting an example for us, giving us hope that we could experience joy under the worst of circumstances, and our joy could lead us to serve.

After Jesus served His disciples, they went to the garden of Gethsemane to pray. Jesus was so distraught and stressed that He was literally sweating blood. But as the crowd came to arrest Him, His actions and words revealed He had peace about Him.

In Hebrews, we're reminded of the joy Jesus felt as He willingly endured the cross. A joy in the fact that He was serving all of humanity with love and salvation.

Isn't it wonderful that our worst moments can be our best if we put our focus on Jesus and others? True joy is available through Jesus and multiplied as we produce fruit by serving others.

Choosing JOY

Meditate on Hebrews 12:2 and ask God how your joy can increase as you find the opportunity to serve in His name and for His glory.

Then he said to them, "Go your way, eat the fat, drink the sweet, and send portions to those for whom nothing is prepared; for this day is holy to our Lord. Do not sorrow, for the joy of the LORD is your strength."

NEHEMIAH 8:10

day eight

JOY BRINGS STRENGTH

Nehemiah was the cupbearer for the Persian king Artaxerxes. The king noticed he was down one day and asked him why. Nehemiah explained how his people in Jerusalem were in great distress and the city was in ruins.

Nehemiah asked to take a leave of absence to rebuild the walls of the city, and his request was granted. Nehemiah went to Jerusalem, organized the project, and they rebuilt the wall in only fifty-two days (Nehemiah 6:15).

The project was wildly successful, but they ran into serious problems along the way. The other people in the region did not want to see a strong Jerusalem and plotted several times to stop the rebuilding. By the grace of God and under Nehemiah's leadership, all of the harmful plans against them were defeated.

What was the secret to their success under such adverse conditions? Joy gave them strength. The work was hard, the threats were real, but doing God's work gave them His joy. And His joy gave them strength.

After the project was completed, they celebrated. They read the Law out loud to all of the people and celebrated with great feasts according to Mosaic law. They still had more work to do to restore Jerusalem to its former greatness, but Nehemiah encouraged them, *"Do not sorrow, for the joy of the* Lord *is your strength"* (Nehemiah 8:10).

When you let God's joy fill you to the fullest, you too can experience supernatural strength to overcome your trials and thrive in His grace. This joy is multiplied as it gives you strength to share it with others.

Choosing JOY

Meditate on Nehemiah 8:10 and ask God to fill you with the kind of joy that gives you strength to overcome any challenges you are facing.

Rejoice in the Lord always.

Again I will say, rejoice!

―――

PHILIPPIANS 4:4

day nine

JOY IN GOD'S PROMISES

Paul was nearing the end of his life when he wrote his letter to the church at Philippi. He had experienced imprisonment and abuse from the Jewish and Roman leaders for his faith. But in the midst of his circumstances, he was full of joy.

Even as he was in prison in Rome, he wrote, *"Rejoice in the Lord always!"*

How did he have so much joy under such terrible circumstances? He had experienced the fulfillment of many of God's promises and completely trusted in them.

God had delivered Paul from the brink of death many times, including multiple shipwrecks, beatings, and imprisonments (2 Corinthians 11:25). God rescued, protected, and restored him as promised.

Paul urged us to rejoice in all things, and he lived his life in Jesus Christ, reflecting God's faithfulness and joy in His promises. Later in that same letter to Philippi, Paul says, *"I seek the fruit that abounds to your account"* and *"I am full"* and *"my God shall supply all your need"* to *"our God and Father be glory forever"*(Philippians 4:17–20).

Paul found joy as God kept His promises. Paul lived with joy as a fruit of the Spirit, in spite of his trials.

God rewarded Paul by miraculously rescuing him multiple times, giving him peace in the midst of his struggles, and filling him with the joy promised by God. We still experience the fruits of Paul's joy.

Choosing JOY

Meditate on Philippians 4:4 and find the promises in His Word about your circumstances, freeing you to rejoice.

Rejoice always, pray without ceasing, in everything give thanks; for this is the will of God in Christ Jesus for you.

---

1 THESSALONIANS 5:16–18

day ten

JOY IS GREATER WITH GRATITUDE

In Paul's last days, while a prisoner in Rome, he wrote a letter to the church at Philippi. He loved the people and was extremely grateful for all they had done for the larger church and for him.

The central theme of Paul's letter is the joy of Jesus. He experiences this joy in his trials. He experiences this joy as he lifts up and encourages his friends in the church. He is so excited about the power of joy, he tells them to "rejoice" nine times in his letter.

Rejoice in the Lord. Rejoice in unity. Rejoice in each other. Rejoice in the sharing of the gospel.

Rejoice in thanksgiving. *"Rejoice in the Lord always. Again I will say, rejoice"* (Philippians 4:4).

Paul begins his letter by giving thanks for the church. He reminds them that he loves them and that he prays for them continually. When he closes out the letter, he expresses deep gratitude again.

Paul also revealed a remarkable truth that thanksgiving is one of the most important aspects of prayer to God: *"Be anxious for nothing, but in everything by prayer and supplication, with thanksgiving, let your requests be made known to God"* (Philippians 4:6).

Joy is important. When you choose joy, your prayers are more intimate. When you choose joy, your gratitude becomes universal. When you choose joy, you are able to focus on the many blessings you have received from God.

When you choose joy, you are able to bring your troubles to God, give Him thanks for your joy, and experience *"the peace of God, which surpasses all understanding"* (Philippians 4:7). When you choose joy, your gratitude is a fruit that encourages those around you.

JOY IS GREATER WITH GRATITUDE

Choosing JOY

Meditate on 1 Thessalonians 5:16–18 and ask God to reveal the abundance of blessings you have to be thankful for that contribute to your joy.

But let all who take refuge in you be glad; let them ever sing for joy. Spread your protection over them, that those who love your name may rejoice in you.

PSALM 5:11 NIV

day eleven

JOY IS A CHOICE

I want to encourage you!
I've talked for a few days now about joy being a *gift* and a *choice*. It's available and free, but you have to choose to accept it, to embrace it, and to receive it.

Every day, you must choose joy. Have you been choosing that joy?

The devil does not want you to have joy. He wants to distract you from God's presence. He will remind you of everything that is wrong, of every sin in the past, of how others have wronged you, and anything else to get you out of God's presence.

But I want to congratulate you. You are doing one of the best things you can do to stay in God's presence and rebuke the devil. You are spending time with Him as you read these Scriptures and this devotional.

I don't know what time of day you are reading this right now, but it doesn't matter. God touched your heart and beckoned you to these pages, based on the hope of the joy He has for you.

When you are feeling great about your day or when you are troubled, pray. Read God's Word. Find a resource that can offer encouragement and help you go deeper in the presence of God.

As God speaks to your heart, embrace Him. Hold Him tight and let His love wash over you. Choose His joy, receive His joy, and experience the fullness of all the joy He has to give you, bearing fruit for those around you.

Choosing JOY

Meditate on Psalm 5:11 and ask God to give you the wisdom and the strength to keep on choosing the fullness of the joy He has for you.

A wise son brings joy to his father, but a foolish man despises his mother.

PROVERBS 15:20 NIV

day twelve

JOY IS FOR THE WHOLE FAMILY

God has a special anointing of joy for your family. I know not all family situations are ideal. My friend Francis Hunter used to say, "Families are like fruitcakes, mostly sweet with a few nuts."

There may be someone in your family who does not have the fullness of joy Jesus offers. They may be a source of concern or anxiety. But families should not be about bringing each other down but instead lifting each other up.

My father had a mental breakdown, and for much of my life, I was concerned that something similar may happen to me. But I chose to receive the joy of the Lord and He told me, "Marilyn, you will not have a mental breakdown."

When I became sick with a parasite, the devil tried to steal my joy. He tried to sink me into depression, reminding me of my father. I held on to the promises of God, which gave me hope, because I chose joy.

Joy for your family must start somewhere. Why not you? When the devil tries to plant seeds of depression or dissatisfaction in your family, go on the offensive. Rejoice in the Lord, embrace an attitude of gratitude, rebuke the devil and his attempt to steal joy from your family, and praise God for His abundant blessings.

Choosing joy for your family calls on the infinite power of God to overcome any circumstances. Choosing joy can change the atmosphere in the present. When you continually choose joy, you can bear fruit in your family for generations.

Choosing JOY

Meditate on Proverbs 15:20 and ask God to help you choose joy for you and your family.

Now may the God of hope fill you with all joy and peace in believing, that you may abound in hope by the power of the Holy Spirit.

ROMANS 15:13

day thirteen

JOY IS LIFE-CHANGING

Saul loved God, and He loved God's Word, but He did not love Jesus . . . at first. Saul was so zealous to defend God and the law of Moses that he rejected what he and the religious leaders believed was a false prophet. He actively pursued arresting and punishing followers of Jesus.

He even held the coats of some of the people who stoned Stephen to death for His faith (Acts 7:58). Stephen was the first recorded Christian to die as a martyr for Jesus.

Saul was traveling to Damascus to arrest more Christians when Jesus appeared to him in light shining from heaven. Jesus asked Saul, *"Why are you persecuting Me?"* (Acts 9:4). Saul asked who He was, and Jesus told him, *"I am Jesus, whom you are persecuting"* (Acts 9:5).

Jesus had chosen Saul for a very special purpose, and Saul converted to Christianity, becoming one of the church leaders and the writer of many of the letters that make up our New Testament. Jesus changed his name to Paul and changed his life forever.

In Paul's letter to the church at Rome, Paul reveals the source of this dramatic change in his life to be God filling him *"with all joy and peace in believing"* (Romans 15:13). He goes on to tell how, as a minister of Jesus Christ to the gentiles, he has reason to glory in Jesus.

When you choose Jesus, you are able to receive the fullness of joy in Him. As you let Him lead you and guide you, your life will change. The changes in your life become your calling in how you will serve Him, and as you bear fruit, your joy is multiplied.

Choosing JOY

Meditate on Romans 15:13 and ask God to change you into the person He created you to be, in the joy He has for you.

And the ransomed of the LORD shall return, and come to Zion with singing, with everlasting joy on their heads. They shall obtain joy and gladness, and sorrow and sighing shall flee away.

ISAIAH 35:10

day fourteen

JOY IS CONTAGIOUS

When God called me to cover the earth with His Word, He put a very strong burden on my heart to bring people to know Him. The desire to help others experience the joy of salvation was insatiable.

I've been blessed beyond measure by this gift of service and joy. I've literally traveled all over the world, including countries that are hostile to Jesus, women, or in many cases, both. But God always paved the road ahead of me.

God had a plan from the beginning of my calling. I was able to speak to large crowds, pray with millions of God's precious souls, and experience great joy as God moved in the lives of those we encountered.

Throughout my ministry, I have always looked for "divine appointments" everywhere I went.

I cannot count the number of times I was able to minister to someone or pray with them in the most unusual settings, like on airplanes, in hotel lobbies, or in the midst of crowds.

God knew the needs of those I encountered and arranged for our meeting. I only had to choose His joy and be ready to share it with whoever I met.

Jesus's joy in you is contagious. You can never be too full of His joy, and it will overflow to those around you if you let it. Sometimes, even if you're not trying. As your joy flows over to others, you bear more fruit, and your joy will continue to increase.

Choosing JOY

Meditate on Isaiah 35:10 and ask God to show you how to share His love and joy so that their sorrow will flee away.

"The LORD your God in your midst, the Mighty One, will save; He will rejoice over you with gladness, He will quiet you with His love, He will rejoice over you with singing."

ZEPHANIAH 3:17

day fifteen

GOD REJOICES OVER YOU

One of God's most endearing qualities is joy. He lives in a perpetual state of joy – it is who He is. We are made in His image; therefore, we are made to experience His joy, and He wants us to live in His joy. In fact, God celebrates when we come into His joy.

Jesus tells three parables in the 15th chapter of Luke that you may remember. First, Jesus tells of the shepherd who had 100 sheep and one of them went missing. He left the 99 alone for a while as he searched for the one that was lost. When he found that sheep, he had great joy and shared the news with his friends and neighbors.

Second, He tells of a woman who had 10 silver coins but lost one. She searched day and night until she found it, and then could not contain her joy as she shared the news with her friends.

Lastly, He tells of a son who lived a wild, sinful life and returned to his father as a servant. When the father spotted him off in the distance returning home, he ran, hugged him, and threw a huge feast for him.

God shares that same joy when one of us is saved. The angels rejoice (Luke 15:10), He *"will rejoice over you with gladness"* (Zephaniah 3:17), and He sends the Holy Spirit to you so that you may be filled with His joy.

Where does the miraculous, life-changing, fruit-bearing joy we get come from? It comes from God Himself, as He experiences it over you and shares the fullness of it with you.

GOD REJOICES OVER YOU

Choosing JOY

Meditate on Zephaniah 3:17 and ask God to help you experience the great joy He has in you.

Those who dwell at the ends of the earth are in awe at your signs. You make the going out of the morning and the evening to shout for joy.

PSALM 65:8 ESV

day sixteen

JOY IS REVEALED IN SIGNS AND WONDERS

God has never stopped being in the miracle business. He delights in showing off with signs, wonders, and miracles as evidence of His goodness, His love for us, and His joy.

When Moses led the Jewish people out of Egypt, it was not easy. God had to deliver 10 plagues, signs, and wonders of His great power before Pharaoh finally agreed to let them leave.

They didn't get far before Pharaoh changed his mind and sent a mighty army of soldiers and chariots to force the Jewish people back into slavery. They were at the edge of the Red Sea when they saw Pharaoh's army in pursuit.

God took the opportunity to show off in a big way. He formed a pillar of cloud to keep the Egyptians from getting too close. Then He parted the Red Sea so that the Jewish people could walk across on dry land. When they reached the other side, God released the waters and destroyed the Egyptian army.

Imagine the joy of God's chosen people as they stood on the far banks of the Red Sea. They had seen miracle after miracle, and finally their salvation from the Egyptians forever.

God gets great joy and extends great joy in His miracles. The psalmist says even the coming and going of morning and evening are great signs to cause a shout for joy (Psalm 65:8).

God can perform His miracles through you, too. Choose to rest fully in His joy and be ready when He calls you to help Him show off and bear fruit for His glory.

Choosing JOY

Meditate on Psalm 65:8 and ask God to guide you into opportunities for Him to perform miracles, great or small, through your joy.

Restore to me the joy of Your salvation, and uphold me by Your generous Spirit.

PSALM 51:12

day seventeen

JOY IN REPENTANCE

King David messed up. He had an affair, and Bathsheba became pregnant with his baby. He had Bathsheba's husband, Uriah, one of his faithful warriors, killed in battle to try and cover it up. His sins hurt several people deeply, and his sins created separation from God. He was miserable.

For a while, he thought he could escape the consequences of his horrible actions, but God would not let him rest in his misery. He missed God, and God missed him.

God told His prophet, Nathan, about David's transgressions, and Nathan confronted David. David confessed his crimes to Nathan and to God.

As the gravity of his crimes caught up to him, the earthly consequences were devastating.

The baby Bathsheba conceived in the affair died. David's kingdom began to crumble.

Then David repented. His earthly life was chaotic, but he was able to experience joy in his heart as he reconnected with God.

Confess your transgressions to God and experience the joy He has for you in freedom. Sins are a burden to carry, but Jesus died on the cross to take that burden away. Sins may result in earthly consequences, but the joy of God overcomes all.

Choosing JOY

Meditate on Psalm 51:12 and ask God to reveal any areas of your life that may be causing separation, so that you may confess and experience restoration and the fullness of His joy He wants for you.

And the word of the Lord was being spread throughout all the region. But the Jews stirred up the devout and prominent women and the chief men of the city, raised up persecution against Paul and Barnabas, and expelled them from their region. But they shook off the dust from their feet against them, and came to Iconium. And the disciples were filled with joy and with the Holy Spirit.

ACTS 13:49-52

day eighteen

JOY IN SHARING THE GOSPEL

Paul and Barnabas were blessed by church elders, had hands laid on them with prayers, and set out to preach the gospel. They traveled to several Mediterranean islands and ended up at Antioch in Pisidia. There was a Jewish community there, so Paul and Barnabas began preaching at the synagogue on the Sabbath.

After the reading of the Law and the Prophets, they eloquently laid out the gospel. They began with the Mosaic law, tracing through the prophecies, explaining how Jesus was the Messiah.

They told how God raised Jesus from the dead and how He appeared to His disciples and other witnesses in Jerusalem and Galilee. They cited Old Testament Scriptures fulfilled by Jesus.

When the Jews left the synagogue, the gentiles in the area begged Paul and Barnabas to share the gospel with them too. The joy of Paul and Barnabas was contagious.

On the next Sabbath, almost the entire city came to hear the gospel. The gentiles were excited and glorified the Word of God, and many others were saved. But some of the Jews were deceived by the devil and were jealous.

Paul and Barnabas boldly shared the gospel. They faced a mixture of excitement and persecution, but they preached anyway. Eventually, they were expelled from the region.

Paul, Barnabas, and the disciples were able to share the gospel all over the Holy Land, *"filled with joy and with the Holy Spirit"* (Acts 13:52).

When you choose the fullness of joy offered by Jesus, your joy is multiplied as you share the gospel with anyone who will hear it.

Choosing JOY

Meditate on Acts 13:49–52 and ask God where your joy can be multiplied as you share His gospel with someone who needs to hear it.

"*I delight to do your will, O my God; your law is within my heart.*"

PSALM 40:8 ESV

day nineteen

JOY IS BEING IN GOD'S WILL

Joy is being in God's will. Many people believe that being in God's will is about following a long set of rules of dos and don'ts. God's will is really so much more.

God had an amazing plan for David. From the time he was anointed while just a shepherd, he had great joy in God's will. He wrote many psalms while he was a shepherd, and he had great success fighting the enemies of Israel while Saul was king, even though Saul was often out to get him.

When he became king, David had great joy leading Israel in the ways of God. As he established Jerusalem as the capital, he brought the ark of the covenant to Jerusalem, restoring it to the place where God met with His people. This was a joyous time for Israel with great celebration.

When David messed up with Bathsheba, he had a period of time when his joy was not so great. But Nathan helped him get back into the will of God, and his joy was restored.

When you choose joy, God promises the fullness of His joy in you. When you are in His will, that joy becomes active as you do what He created you to do, for your pleasures, His purposes, and His glory.

When you have the fullness of God's joy and are in His will, you become stronger, more powerful, and a bolder voice for the gospel of Jesus. Your joy multiplies as it overflows across God's path for your life.

Choosing JOY

Meditate on Psalm 40:8 and ask God to help you find your joy in the comfort of His perfect will for you.

Make a joyful shout to the LORD, all you lands! Serve the LORD with gladness; come before His presence with singing. Know that the LORD, He is God; it is He who has made us, and not we ourselves; we are His people and the sheep of His pasture.

PSALM 100:1-3

day twenty

JOY IN WORSHIP

When David was young, he was a shepherd. Other than keeping the sheep gathered around him and fighting off lions and bears, he had a lot of time on his hands. This was a very special time for David.

While David was in the fields with his sheep, he spent a lot of time in prayer and worship. He loved God, and he loved to be with Him. He was so full of the joy of the Lord he had to express it.

David wrote more psalms in the Bible than any other writer. Many of them were written to music. David played the harp and other stringed instruments. He had a reputation for his worship and talent as a musician.

Saul was inflicted with an evil spirit after he disobeyed God, and his joy was gone. When he was in a foul mood, he would call on David to come and worship God in his presence with his harp. It always changed Saul's mood.

David was a man after God's own heart. He was so full of God's joy it overflowed in praise and worship. I can't say for certain that David was full of joy *so* he worshiped, or full of joy *because* he worshiped... but the two come together in the songs of David.

When you choose joy, raise your hands and your voice in worship to God. When you are struggling to find the fullness of God's joy, raise your hands and voice in worship to God. It is difficult not to feel the joy of God when you are truly lost in worship, and your joy will overflow to those you encounter.

Choosing JOY

Meditate on Psalm 100:1–3 and spend some time in God's presence, worshiping Him from the depths of your heart, letting Him fill you with His joy.

"Let us be glad and rejoice and give Him glory, for the marriage of the Lamb has come, and His wife has made herself ready."

REVELATION 19:7

day twenty-one

JOY IS ETERNAL IN THE SECOND COMING OF JESUS

After the fall of Adam and Eve, life was not going to be the same for us. We were born into sin and had to choose to let the joy of God find its fullness in us. The Bible is largely the story of this struggle, from joy to sorrow and then back to joy.

God established the law for a long time as a means to atone for our sins and get the joy of God back in our lives. But God had a much bigger, much better plan. He was so eager for us to restore our relationship with Him, that He was ready to make a sacrifice on our behalf.

God made the ultimate sacrifice when He sent His Son to die for our sins on that cross. Jesus made a way for us to be intimate with God once again, to be full of His joy, and to bear the fruits of our joy.

But His plan was still not complete. It would get even bolder, bigger, and more glorious. God is going to send Jesus to us one more time. Not just in our hearts, but as a Holy Warrior, coming to defeat sin once and for all and restore His joy in us for eternity.

Jesus told His disciples He would come again and gave some strong hints about how to know when the time was coming soon. John wrote the book of Revelation to describe His second coming as a Bridegroom coming for His bride.

Choose the fullness of God's joy now. Let yourself get caught up in worship, thanksgiving, praise, and song. Share this joy with everyone God tells you to. Jesus is coming again, and what a joy that will be!

JOY IS ETERNAL IN THE SECOND COMING OF JESUS

Choosing JOY

Meditate on Revelation 19:7 and ask God to prepare you for His coming, for His joy, for an eternity with Him.

I'VE GOT THE JOY

VERSE 1

I've got the joy, joy, joy, joy down in my heart
Where?
Down in my heart!
Where?
Down in my heart!
I've got the joy, joy, joy, joy down in my heart
Down in my heart to stay

CHORUS

And I'm so happy, so very happy
I've got the love of Jesus in my heart
And I'm so happy, so very happy
I've got the love of Jesus in my heart.

Verse 2

I've got the love of Jesus,
    love of Jesus down in my heart
Where?
Down in my heart!
Where?
Down in my heart!
I've got the love of Jesus,
    love of Jesus down in my heart
Where?
Down in my heart to stay.
Repeat Chorus

Verse 3

And if the Devil doesn't like it he can sit on a tack!
Ouch!
Sit on a tack!
Ouch!
Sit on a tack!
And if the Devil doesn't like it he can sit on a tack!
Ouch!
Sit on a tack to stay!
Repeat Chorus to finish

ADDITIONAL VERSE

I've got the wonderful love of my blessed Redeemer deep down in the depths of my heart.
Where?
Down in the depths of my heart!
Where?
Down in the depths of my heart!
I've got the wonderful love of my blessed Redeemer deep down in the depths of my heart.
Where?
Down in the depths of my heart to stay!

Repeat Chorus to finish

George W. Cooke, "I've Got the Joy." Public Domain.

ABOUT MARILYN

*E*ncouraging, optimistic, always upbeat and energetic, even in her later years, Marilyn Hickey actively ministers internationally. As founder and president of *Marilyn & Sarah Ministries*, a non-profit ministry and humanitarian organization based in Denver, Colorado, Marilyn has traveled to over 140 countries and has impacted many nations around the world – from disaster relief efforts in Haiti, Indonesia, and Pakistan to providing food for the hungry in Mexico, Costa Rica, Russia, and the Philippines.

Her legacy includes significant ministry in Islamic countries. In 2016, over one million people attended her healing meeting in Karachi, Pakistan.

Marilyn has held audiences with government leaders and heads of state all over the world. She was the first woman to join the board of directors for Dr. David Yonggi Cho (founder of the world's largest congregation, Yoido Full Gospel Church in South Korea).

Along with her daughter, pastor Sarah Bowling, she co-hosts the daily television program, *Today with Marilyn & Sarah*, which is broadcast globally in nearly 200 countries with a potential viewing audience of over 2 billion households worldwide. Marilyn has also authored over 100 publications.

She and her late husband, Wallace, were married over 50 years and had two children and five grandchildren. Marilyn holds a Bachelor of Arts in Collective Foreign Languages from the University of Northern Colorado and an Honorary Doctor of Divinity from Oral Roberts University.

In 2015, Marilyn was honored at Oral Roberts University with the prestigious Lifetime Global Achievement Award. This award recognizes individuals, or organizations, that have made a significant impact in the history of ORU and around the world. In 2019, Marilyn also received an International Lifetime Peace Award from the Grand Imam and President of Pakistan.

In 2021, Marilyn was honored with two awards from the Assemblies of God Theological Seminary: The Pillar of Faith Award in acknowledgment of her worldwide impact on the church through biblical teaching and sustainable healing ministry; and the Smith Wigglesworth Award, given on behalf of the entire Assemblies of God fellowship in acknowledgment of her decades of service worldwide.

Marilyn's greatest passion and desire is to continue being a bridge-builder in countries around the world, and she shows no signs of stopping.

To Learn More About
Marilyn & Sarah Ministries, Visit:

Marilyn & Sarah Ministries: **marilynandsarah.org**
Check out our free downloads that include Bible reading plans, teaching notes, inspirational graphics, spiritual self-assessments, and lists of verses based on topic.

Online Master Classes: **mentoredbymarilyn.org**
Marilyn is passing her mantle on to you! Through her anointed master classes, you will be mentored in strategic areas that will take you to the next level of victory and fulfillment in your life and ministry. This is an incredible opportunity to be mentored by Marilyn!

Connect with Marilyn:
- MarilynHickeyMinistries
- MarilynandSarah
- MarilynHickeyMinistries
- MarilynHickeyMinistries